VANISHED!
How to
PROTECT YOURSELF
and YOUR CHILDREN

A simple and inexpensive step-by-step guide

By L. Ives

Copyright 2012 by Leon Ives

All rights to this book and all manuscripts are reserved by the owner and author. No part of this book shall be reproduced, stored in a retrieval system, or transmitted by any means, electronic, mechanical, photocopying, or otherwise, without written permission from the owner, except in the case of brief quotations in articles and reviews. Excerpts may also be used in training and education with the proper citation. Permission is not required for individuals producing the Individual Protection Packet and Biographical Form for personal use.

For permission, please contact Leon Ives with GBP Consulting, Investigative & Security Services, Inc. at www.GBPServicesInc.com.

ISBN-13: 978-1477453599
ISBN-10: 1477453598
LCCN: 2012908728
BISAC: Self-Help / General

Testimonials

Leon Ives has taken his many years of experience in law enforcement, combined it with chilling statistics and accounts of crimes against innocent victims, and put together the one book that is a must-read for any parent. Each day we see reports in the news about unfathomable crimes and incidents against innocent children, women, men, and families. The victims rarely realize that what is about to happen to them, will happen. Being prepared and being able to react quickly and properly greatly enhances the odds of a happy ending. Leon's book paves the path to ensuring all of us can do all in our power to safeguard and protect our families. Kudos to him for sharing this valuable information with all of us!

LtCol Bill Cowan, USMC (Ret)
Fox News Contributor
Co-founder and CEO of WVC3, Inc. in Virginia
Specializing in International Security and Intelligence

Leon Ives, a decorated, experienced federal agent and military advisor has captured, developed and reported a must read road map for the protection and preservation of each family's most valuable asset, "Our Children". "Vanished" outlines simple steps in the event horrific crimes are committed against the children of the world. This book is full of solid advice backed up by cold hard facts that law enforcement officers have been putting together and practicing for years; and now it is available to parents outlining basic rules, advanced tactics, and emergency procedures. Mr. Ives has dedicated his life to doing the right thing, whether protecting society from criminal organizations or protecting the innocent in war-torn countries.

Tom Hancock
Director - Financial Economic Crimes
ING Direct Bank of Canada
Retired Police Detective of the Toronto Police Service (Canada) with 30 years' experience

Do not ignore this book! What can I do to protect my children? As a parent and grandparent this thought has been with me for all my for 30 years law enforcement service, and continues into retirement with my private work for custody cases, child protection, and due diligence on potential new partners and boy/girlfriends. This book will tell you how to adopt the knowledge of the author and other experts. Pedophiles are in our community, some known, many not. They plot and plan: learn how to prevent and counter an attack on your child. Leon Ives has the experience and knowledge to put you the necessary steps ahead. There is page after page of solid advice. This is stuff that law enforcement officers have been putting together and practicing for years, and now it is available to parents. It gives you basic rules, advanced tactics, and emergency procedures to follow. I have a background in local, national, and international child protection; and border policing. I give my professional endorsement to this book.

Nigel Wilkinson
Detective Chief Inspector, Ret
United Kingdom

Leon Ives has created a safety bible for protecting children and loved ones. His Individual Protection Packets contain easy-to-follow instructions, and crucial details that will help law enforcement accelerate the pace of their search. Awareness, knowledge, and security planning are the best way to prevent, deter, and delay intrusions from the evil amongst us. Leon takes you inside the mind of an investigator who is conducting a missing person investigation. After reading *Vanished* you will know exactly what information law enforcement needs to help find your loved ones as quickly as possible. There is no doubt in my mind that the insight gleaned from Leon Ives and *Vanished* will help diminish pain and save lives.

Steve Neal
Leatherman-Neal, LLC
Law Enforcement Leadership
Chester, VA
Former Police Commander and Public Safety University Director

Being a victim is something one may not recognize until you are suddenly caught in a situation that requires you to think and react quickly. The resources and information in Leon Ives' book "Vanished! How to Protect Yourself and Your Children" are crucial to a favorable outcome. Understanding the threat and protecting yourself and your family is an imperative element for avoidance of such issues. Leon, you have put together one of the most valuable resources every family should have, thank you for your hard work, time, and dedication to help others become empowered to avoid or overcome situations that most feel could never happen to them. The threats are real, the perpetrators are constantly lurking, and the power of knowing is what keeps up alive and well. God Bless.

Dana Way, CMI-V, CCI, CI, DABCCI, CFC
Chief Association Officer
American College of Forensic Examiners Institute
American Association of Integrative Medicine
American Psychotherapy Association

An absolute MUST read for parents. The material in this guide has been meticulously researched, and if followed, has the potential to save the lives of children and protect families. The provided statistics are numbing, and as a parent, jump-started my efforts to protect those that I love. The Biographical form and the Individual Protection Packet are essential to law enforcement's first few hours of investigation. Read this book, parents, and make additional copies available to friends and relatives as a birthday or holiday present. It will be the best present you could give.

Bill Gonzalez
Virginia
Former Federal Law Enforcement Agent

Leon Ives has masterfully written this book to guide, teach, and protect our loved ones, especially the most vulnerable – our children. As a law enforcement officer and parent, I believe the information in this book will reduce the risks of our family and friends falling prey to predators.

David M. Marwell
Texas
Federal Criminal Investigator with 25 years of experience.

Vanished! A must read for any parent in America. A truly informative guideline to assist others in the event a loved one goes missing. Leon Ives outlines a proven plan in his book to get fast results and save lives. The book should be in every home in America in the event that the unthinkable occurs. Definitely a great resource for everyone.

Dana Blount-Piatt
Retired FBI Investigative Specialist
Atlanta, GA
President of MarketComm

Parents are both advocates and protectors for their children. *Vanished!*, by former Special Agent Leon Ives, serves as a road map and battle plan for parents. One should not attempt to navigate hostile territory without a comprehensive Operational Plan. This thorough and detailed guide is not only for parents, but for those who seek to protect all their love ones who live in a hostile world.

David Tinsley
CEO of 5 Stones Intelligence
Miami, FL
Global intelligence and investigative operations
Former Drug Enforcement Administration Supervisory Special Agent

Mr. Ives' book is an outstanding resource for families before, during or after dealing with the disappearance of a loved one. It is also a great read for investigators. Each chapter of this book provides invaluable information to families in their time of need. Because of countless violent crimes, missing- person cases are not often given high priority by law enforcement officials. More and more families are turning to private investigators and other professionals for assistance. I would highly recommend this book to all families and investigators alike.

Gary Pastor
Owner of Private Eyes, Inc.
Greenville, NC
President of the North Carolina Association of Private Investigators (NCAPI)

Kudos to the author who cared enough to write this safety net for children. As a private investigator for almost 18 years, specializing in Family Law Investigations, hearing an Amber Alert by far echoes the most gut wrenching feeling second only to a death. As a mother of two and a grandmother of three…almost four…it is truly my biggest fear! Two words come to mind after reading this book, "Thank God!"

Pat Sauls
Pat Sauls Investigative Services
Publisher of "On the Record" magazine
Raleigh, NC

★★★★★

In a world where the unexpected occurs constantly, it is a must to be prepared for the worse. This book will get you prepared, and should be on the bookshelf of every household.

Will Williams
Author of Happier Ever After
Raleigh, NC
Financial Services

★★★★★

As a veteran with 40 years' experience in criminal investigation, seeing the dark side of human nature, I highly recommend "Vanished!" as a must read for all families. This book is a template that will teach you awareness of your surroundings and skills to make sure of a positive outcome.

Please read, learn, and practice what is spelled out in this outline for survival.

William Henderson
President. OBN Security & Investigative Consultants
Toronto, Canada

Dedications

This book is dedicated with love and sympathy to both the victims and their families who have suffered unimaginable pain and grief through a disappearance. For those who are still missing, you will remain in our prayers.

This book is also dedicated to the men and women of law enforcement and firefighters; and those who serve in our military forces and national intelligence community. These are America's warriors—the courageous guardians who risk life and injury to defend our great country and our communities. Many have sacrificed much so that we can remain safe. This dedication also includes all the emergency medical personnel who take personal risks as well, so that we may continue to enjoy life.

A special appreciation is extended to the employees and volunteers at the National Center for Exploited and Missing Children, Let's Bring Them Home, and all the other missing-persons organizations who support us. There are too many to name. Thank you for your service.

Last, but not least, this book is dedicated to my family and friends who have supported and sustained me over the years, making me a better person. It has taken a lot of work, hasn't it? Thank you and I love you all. Welcome to the family Michael.

Author's Comments

For simplicity I will use either *female or male*, but typically I am referring to both genders. I may refer to protecting our "children," but I am also speaking of teenagers, adults, and the elderly. In the world of peril and safety, our children, women, and elderly are the most vulnerable and precious. Let's keep them safe.

I will use the words *police officer, detective* and *police department*, but I am including all law enforcement officers and police investigators at the city, county, state, and federal levels. The same applies to the word *government*.

I am very proud of America's law enforcement and government. As our nation's guardians and leaders, they are held to a higher standard and they must demonstrate professional work ethics and personal integrity every step of the way. I truly appreciate those dedicated and honest officers, officials, and politicians who unselfishly serve our great country, communities, and the People—the most important part of America.

We are a great nation of incredibly strong, brave, and charitable people. Others all over the world admire and emulate Americans—some secretly in order to survive. I have met thousands of such individuals in more than twenty different countries, and every day someone said, "Thank you. Thank you, America!"

The information I provide may seem redundant at times. That's okay. There is so much information to share and contemplate that redundancy may be necessary. This is an informational guide. Just ignore my writing style and mistakes. I'm not a professional writer by any means. ***It is the message and the advice that are important.***

Various statistics and numbers were taken from official websites, studies, reports, et cetera, found on the Internet. The exact figures are irrelevant;

it is the sheer magnitude of these various problems that matter. ***It is the threat we must understand and learn to fight.***

My background includes over thirty-nine years of experience in the United States Army and Army Reserve, as well as in the federal government under the legacy US Customs Service, Office of Investigations; and the Department of Homeland Security, Homeland Security Investigations. My career fields included law enforcement, counterintelligence, civil-military affairs, and criminal investigations. I have worked in the private security sector for the past seven years as a professional consultant, private investigator, security specialist, and trainer/mentor.

In the course of my careers, I have lived and traveled to numerous states and cities throughout the US; as well as over twenty foreign countries. I have seen the good in people, as well as the bad. I have discovered what criminals know and how they think. I have learned a lot about personal, physical, and national security. My goal and desire is to share my knowledge and experiences in order to teach you and others how to protect yourselves and those you love. This book is packed with professional and personal advice.

Disclaimer: Numerous missing-persons organizations will be named throughout this book. I am not affiliated with any of these organizations or businesses. Their information is provided for your knowledge and for use as a resource.

Vanished! How to Protect Yourself and Your Children

Table of Contents

Chapter 1	Introduction	1
Chapter 2:	General Information	17
Chapter 3:	Hiring a Private Investigator	69
Chapter 4:	Statistics and Numbers to Think About	77
Chapter 5:	Become an Advocate for Missing-persons	97
Chapter 6:	Personal Awareness and Prevention	109
Chapter 7:	The Internet	147
Chapter 8:	Physical Security	153
Chapter 9:	Your Emergency Identification Card	163
Chapter 10:	Your Individual Protection Packets	169
Chapter 11:	The Biographical Form	183
Chapter 12:	Abbreviated Individual Protection Packet	193
Chapter 13:	Basic Rules to Follow	197
Chapter 14:	Personal Security Equipment and Services	215
Chapter 15:	Who to Contact for More Information and Help	221
Chapter 16:	The End	231

Chapter 1

INTRODUCTION

Vanished is a simple and inexpensive step-by-step guide that will teach you how to protect yourself and your loved ones. Learn how to safeguard your *children*, spouse, boyfriend or girlfriend, brothers or sisters, parents, grandparents, and even a close friend.

Our goal is to prevent a missing person incident or a violent attack from happening in the first place. The second goal is to find our loved one as *quickly* as humanly possible. You don't have to be a victim. You can protect a loved one from severe physical and emotional trauma. These heart wrenching occurrences are in fact preventable with just a little effort, time, and money. I'll make it easy for you.

Schools, caregivers, other service providers, and private organizations need to protect their students, customers, and members as well. This informative book can help protect a business or organization from a preventable tragedy and the possibility of a lawsuit for negligence and liability.

This responsibility is called *risk management* and *due diligence.* Always be prepared and exercise the proper caution. For a very brief moment in life, we are entrusting our loved ones into the care of your institution. You too have an obligation to protect our loved ones.

This also applies to the business owners and managers at the places where we work. Protect your employees and customers from this threat and *workplace violence.* Workplace violence is another whole topic to research and learn about.

This book will give you excellent advice and ideas. It will help you start thinking about protecting yourself and your loved ones. It is time to open our eyes and become proactive. The biggest step, after reading this book, is what will you do with what you have learned?

It is a fact of life we unfortunately choose to ignore: thousands of children and adults turn up missing every day. When these disastrous events strike, we must find our loved one as *quickly* as possible, before they are seriously harmed or vanish. Remember that! Find them as quickly as possible. I'll teach you how.

Our loved ones need to be found or rescued in just a few short hours, not twenty-four or forty-eight hours later, and certainly not after days, weeks, or months. By then it might be too late. Every minute a loved one is missing is life-threatening and heartbreaking. The sheer number of missing-person reports makes it a serious strain on law enforcement to always react with complete expediency and thoroughness, but they *must.* We must ensure the authorities do everything possible. We cannot risk the life and welfare of one innocent child or adult. Not one!

People who seem to have vanished have been found years later, so we must never give up our search and our hope. You can prevent this needless pain and suffering if you are willing to take that extra step in establishing a personal or family *security plan.* Again, it's easy and I'll help you.

These are just my terms. A person who is said to have *disappeared* may be missing and a search and investigation have recently been initiated. A person who has *vanished* can be said to be missing, but for a longer period despite efforts to locate them. It may be semantics. A loved one who has turned up missing is very serious matter and every effort needs to be initiated in the beginning to find them immediately. This is not always the case. If someone tells you it has only been twelve or twenty-four hours, smack them on the head. That's like saying someone just started drowning.

It's hard to understand why parents and other people won't take simple precautions. Why suffer the emotional agony of a disappearance? Why suffer the brutality of a violent attack? This is the difficult and troublesome questions we will ask ourselves after the fact: *"What could I have done to prevent this from happening?" "What could I have done to help find my loved one?"*

Is the answer that you don't know what to do? Well, I will teach you. You will soon have the answers and the guidance to hopefully prevent a missing-person tragedy from occurring in the first place. Should this misfortune occur, there will be a viable security plan in place to help find you or your loved one as fast as humanly possible.

Much of what you are about to learn will help protect you from other violent attacks that do not involve disappearances. How's that for a bonus? Learn how to protect yourself and your family at all times.

Let's start with a few thought-provoking scenarios. Think about each of these questions for several minutes and make an honest assessment of how you would react if any of these dreadful situations were to occur. Those of us who have raised children have experienced one or more of these gut-wrenching moments. Panic! Indecision! Take some time and ask yourself, *"What exactly would I do?"*

You are out shopping. You turn around and your younger child has suddenly disappeared. You start calling his name as you frantically search the area, but you cannot find him anywhere.

You come home from work and your child is nowhere to be seen. You figure he is probably somewhere in the neighborhood playing with a friend. By dinner time he has not returned home.

Your wife or husband goes out for the evening with friends, or your teenage daughter goes out on a date. It is well after midnight and you have not heard from them.

Your child is away from home in college or on a foreign vacation. You have not heard from her in a few days, so you try calling. You don't get a response. You call the school officials or the chaperone, but they have no idea where she is. They were going to wait until the next day and then call you or the police. Ouch!

Your parents or grandparents are on a trip and you haven't heard from them. No one in the family knows exactly where they are. They don't answer their cell phones.

Your loved one is missing and the police do not appear to be taking your case seriously, or doing enough to locate her. What can *you* do?

What specific steps would you take in any of these situations? More important, what are some specific steps you could have taken to prevent such occurrences in the first place? Not sure? This book will tell you exactly what you should do and how to do it. After reading this book, come back and answer those questions. The keys to personal security and survival are **Awareness** and **Prevention**.

First, you must understand the potential threats encountered in life by most every person every minute of the day. No one is immune. Some are just lucky that the threats passed them by. Learn how to be aware of your surroundings and identify potential threats. Learn how to assess these possible threats. In the military and law enforcement we call this *situational awareness*.

Second, you must learn specific methods and techniques to protect yourself and your loved ones. Learn how to avoid and prevent tragic incidents from happening in the first place, but also learn what to do should something happen. Learn how to assess potential or actual threats and exercise the appropriate caution or take the proper action. Prevention includes finding a missing loved one as quickly as possible before they are harmed. You may have only moments to react. React with purpose and confidence. We call this *being technically and tactically proficient.*

Here is a dose of reality you may not want to believe—or accept. You live in two worlds: your world and *their* world. What other world am I referring to? It is the world of irrational and uncontainable crime involving violence, drugs, alcohol, sex, and the exploitation of others for perverted desires or money. Madness! The savage animals and sadistic monsters living in this other world are consumed by these vices, and they may consume you.

There are several million *violent criminals* and *sexual predators* in the United States, and we are literally surrounded by them. Many are *pedophiles* preying on our children. Again, their criminal behaviors are predicated on these vices: extreme violence, illegal and pharmaceutical drugs, alcohol abuse, perverted sex, and/or criminal exploitation of people for personal desires or profit.

These are the threats that emanate from that other world, and you are about to learn about each. These are the vices and threats we need to discuss with our children and teenagers. Sit down and communicate with them. Make it a two-way discussion, not a lecture. There are a lot of good materials to help you educate younger children and teenagers. I'll tell you where to find them.

Who are these savage animals and sadistic monsters we must learn to avoid and combat at all cost? You unknowingly cross their paths everywhere you go. They are sometimes hiding in the shadows and often standing right before you—unnoticed and watching. Sometimes they are open and engaging. Some are very charismatic and can easily worm their way into your life. However, their sole purpose in life is to satisfy their addictive cravings and to draw you and your children into *their world.*

These disturbing and deadly predators, sexual or otherwise, are people you have probably met before and think of as being harmless. They may be complete strangers. They may be casual acquaintances you work with or people you occasionally encounter in the neighborhood, at school, while shopping, or during leisure activities. They may be a charming new boyfriend or a casual date you *thought* you could trust. Sometimes they are friends or even family members.

These other people from that other world are mentally disturbed and physically destructive, and they will change and ruin your life forever. They may seem perfectly okay or just a little odd, but they are mentally and behaviorally psychotic (abnormal). They are deviants who enjoy fear and inflicting pain and there are literally millions of them watching and waiting.

I call these criminal psychopaths animals and monsters. A raging and uncontrollable storm lies beneath their surface—sometimes well hidden—but these beasts are always on the prowl. Often you will not recognize them. They hurt and kill others because they need to satisfy their various addictions and cravings. Learn how to spot them.

Understand that psychopaths have varying types and degrees of abnormal personality and behavioral disorders. They do not have morals or a sense of right and wrong. They have absolutely no regard for the laws and rules of a society. They do not perceive long term consequences for their actions or possess true emotions and remorse. Unlike many of my professional brethren who take a purely clinical analysis of these psychotics, I believe they are truly evil. I have met many of them face to face.

They are masters of deception and manipulation. Many demonstrate signs of grandiose behavior or they appear very withdrawn. Some are very charming and others ooze indifference or hatred. Their psychoses are not always diagnosed or understood, so if arrested and convicted of a crime, these antisocial creatures are often released to prey again on an innocent society. Why is this being allowed within our judicial system at such a high number? Good question.

CHAPTER 1: INTRODUCTION

For many of them, their psychological tendencies, addictions, and/or cravings produce irresistible urges and desires they cannot suppress or escape. It is comparable to having an overwhelming thirst or hunger. Most of the monsters who have already attacked once cannot be rehabilitated, but many criminal psychiatrists and psychologists, along with attorneys and judges, think that they can. So, the monsters are released back into society and public to attack again.

These animals and monsters who have brutally attacked or killed innocent people do not deserve a second chance for two reasons: to exact justice for both the victim and their families and more important to protect innocent people and families from future acts of brutality and murder. Our courts do not accept this premise. They believe most anyone can be rehabilitated; therefore, more and more innocent people will suffer every year. One is too many, especially if it is one of your loved ones. Let the punishment fit the crime.

I keep saying animals and monsters. Again, these are my terms. The savage animals are the ones who, without provocation or warning, viciously strike out resulting in serious harm or death. They live by violent terms and will not hesitate to commit a physical assault, including rape. The monsters are predators who intentionally stalk us to fulfill their perverted lust for cruelty, sex, and death. The monsters who have brutally attacked and murdered should never be released back into society. Yet they are. Time and time again.

Once these animals or monsters zero in on you, they begin sizing you up and hatching a plan of deception and violence. You become the focus of their madness. That plan can be spontaneous or may take time to develop. These creatures are both impulsive and calculating. Once they attack it will be with extreme force and often turns to rage and fury. It is what they do. It is their nature. Some are savage animals who strike out and take what they want (if anything) and move on, but some are much worse. Some are monsters who will stalk, capture, and devour with utter viciousness.

It is estimated that **80 percent of "criminally psychopathic" inmates will be arrested again** for some reason, compared to less than half of other inmates. I have seen figures as high as 90 percent. Remember, what I said earlier. It is not the exactness of the figures; it is the sheer enormity of the problem. It really doesn't matter—either figure is too high.

Who cares if nefarious kidnappings occur a thousand times a year, ten thousand, or one hundred thousand times a year? Any of those numbers are simply too high. Why do I provide and report these numbers? There are more to come. Because many jurists and government officials apparently feel these numbers are acceptable considering the immense size of our nation's population. Many of them look at it as percentages and ratios. That is madness!

There are literally millions of *them* in this other world and we cannot avoid them. Millions! I'll provide some statistics later. So, you had better learn to recognize them. What do they look like? They come in all shapes and sizes. They usually appear ordinary and nonthreatening. Some are as young as your children and most are adults of any age. They are both men and women of all races and ethnicities. You don't really see them because you are not looking hard enough and paying close attention. Your focus is elsewhere or your knowledge is limited. Most of us are *good* people. We don't know or really think about these *bad* things.

Law enforcement officers and prosecutors know all about these animals and monsters. So do psychiatrists and psychologists dealing with personality disorders and behavioral issues. In law enforcement this field is referred to as *criminal psychology*. How this issue pertains to the legal system is referred to as *forensics psychology*. Staff members working in jails and prisons around the country interact with them every day. Medical professionals in the various fields of law enforcement and rehabilitation know all about these monsters and their insatiable appetites. Yes, there are millions of them.

CHAPTER 1: INTRODUCTION

This is the other world you live in. This is the other world that your children and teenagers live in as well. They too are encountering animals and monsters of their own age. Many adolescents, from ages ten to nineteen years, have been convicted of extreme acts of cruelty (torture and sex) and cold-blooded murder that are beyond comprehension.

This book will teach you how to protect yourself and your family from these animals and monsters. It will teach you how to recognize and size them up (role reversal). You will learn how to put up effective barriers and defenses to keep them at bay. This must be done at home, work and everywhere else you go. Again, it is not difficult; it just takes a conscious effort. Get to work. What can be more important?

If they should snatch you or a loved one, you need an effective security plan in place that will enable you to find your loved one as quickly as possible—*before* serious harm or death is inflicted. What is the key word here? Right, "before." Do you have an actual plan in place? Do you know what to do? Soon you will. You won't believe how simple and inexpensive it is.

Why should you be worried? Here are some alarming studies and statistics. These numbers are averages and estimates. Again, don't worry about exact figures and ignore those people who will argue over these statistics. Just recognize the numbers are big—way too big! They are both shocking and outrageous for such a modern society with a sound government and technologically advanced law enforcement.

In the United States of America, on average, over 790,000 children and 200,000 adults are reported missing every year. **Together, children and adults total over 990,000 missing-person reports each year, or one person every 32 seconds.** It is estimated those numbers may even reach one million by the end of the year 2012. Wow! That is a staggering number! This is a national epidemic.

What happens to these one million people? Fortunately, some turn up missing as a result of miscommunication and are quickly located unharmed. Whew! Others are involved in accidents, and you may not learn about these mishaps for hours or days. Many children run away, and adults run away as well. Most are found or return home on their own accord within a few days or weeks. But, it will seem like a lifetime. We can learn how to avoid all this.

Unfortunately, many of our loved ones disappear *not* through miscommunication, accidents, or to momentarily escape from problems at home or school. Thousands are kidnapped from their homes or communities, and then they are seriously abused and often murdered. There are different types of kidnappings, including child abductions by estranged parents, we will discuss later. The bottom line: let's learn how to find our loved ones as *quickly* as possible. It can be done if you are prepared.

Some adolescents and adults decide to run away to escape their problems and fall victim to predators. Running away is not a solution, and we need to recognize their frustration and desire to escape. It usually begins with signs of *depression* and self-isolation. It can lead to suicide. Parents need to learn more about these problems through research and professional counseling.

Listen! If you or a loved one appears to suffer from depression, or suicidal thoughts, please seek professional medical treatment and counseling. This is a very serious problem being overlooked by many adults, and the parents of adolescents. Depression is a medical issue that can be diagnosed and treated. It involves overwhelming feelings of unhappiness and hopelessness. Despair! That is no way to live. As Bobby McFerrin sang, "Don't Worry Be Happy." (Or, was that Bob Marley?) Not worrying and being happy are not always easy to do, but it is possible.

Research this topic if you feel this way, or if someone close to you appears to be depressed. Are they always angry or mad? Are they overly quiet or brooding? Are they withdrawing from family and friends? Do they no longer seem to care about anything, to include their appearance, school, or work? Learn more about depression, and what you can do to help yourself or someone you love or care about.

Okay, back on track. When our children or loved ones run away from home, they may be preyed upon by those living in that other world. These innocent victims include individuals of any age—both boys and girls or men and women. This is reality! Every year thousands of children and adults innocently run away and are naively drawn into this other world through *manipulation* or *force*. They become victims of unfathomable mental anguish, torment, and unspeakable horrors. While back at home, hearts are broken and family relationships crumble.

However, many runaways are mentally and emotionally manipulated by these animals and monsters from the start. Again, this includes children and adults. These victims leave home with their future assailant somewhat willingly—at first. They didn't really plan to leave forever. They just wanted to get away, and the manipulator recognized this emotional weakness and took advantage by offering false care and love. The life raft turns out to be an unbearable journey, or a death trap.

That other world has existed since the beginning of time. It is a harsh and forbidding world where good and innocent people are exploited. Some victims die accidently from sexual abuse, beatings, torture, drug overdoses, and dreadful illnesses. Or, they are used and intentionally murdered and discarded like trash. I suppose some die of hopelessness and heartbreak. I cannot comprehend that level of despair. Just giving up and dying. Never give up hope or stop fighting. Always maintain the will to survive.

The information in this book provides excellent advice for avoiding kidnappings (real or perceived) and violent or sexual assaults. Real or perceived—what does that mean? We will learn more. It doesn't really matter if missing-person incidents involve *kidnappings, runaways, accidents, or miscommunication;* we can safeguard against all of those unfortunate events with just a little effort. Yes, I said just a little effort.

Along with valuable information and advice, this book includes instructions on how to prepare your very own **Individual Protection Packets** for yourself and each of your loved ones. These protection packets include a **Biographical Form** that can help both you and the police locate your loved one as fast as possible. All the information you and the police need will be at your fingertips. These protection packets are the *key* to finding your loved one as quickly as possible. They are your real life raft. I am giving this gift to you for the price of this book. Give this gift to someone else you care about.

Crucial advice: It is extremely important to find a missing person in the first *few* hours, before they are seriously harmed or vanish. Don't let anyone tell you it is twenty-four, forty-eight, or seventy-two hours.

What exactly should you do if a loved one turns up missing? Many people are uninformed about these matters and some become too overwhelmed with fear and emotion to react properly. Most people are not trained law enforcement officers and investigators, so they do not know the appropriate steps to take immediately. The trick is to have a plan, which also serves as a thorough *checklist*. Nothing forgotten and nothing missed. Not by you and not by the police. Pretty good idea, right?

Should a loved one unexpectedly turn up missing, you can use the Biographical Form in your protection packets to start contacting dozens of people who know or somehow associates with your loved one. No guessing or wasted hours searching for multiple names, telephone numbers, e-mails, and locations.

You will be able to immediately contact numerous individuals who will likely know where your loved can be found. You may contact an unlikely source who will point you in the right direction. Or, you may inadvertently contact an unlikely suspect. Any of these simple phone calls or messages (emails or texts) may save your loved one's life.

If your loved one turns up missing, use your Biographical Form to start contacting everyone as quickly as possible and spread the word. ***Posters are good, but the lightning speed of text messages and e-mails are much faster.*** What do people do all day? Text and e-mail; and, this can include Facebook and other social sites. By saving special pictures to your smartphone and computer, you can send detailed messages and attach a few photographs. Again, the Biographical Form will provide you with dozens of specific names, cell phone numbers, and e-mail addresses.

I still suggest you have a variety of posters prepared on your computer. I saw one smart poster that along with a full description, it included front and profile facial photographs, as well as a picture of her car and license plate. I would suggest a full body shot as well.

In your text or e-mail, ask those whom you contact to *forward* your message to everyone they know. In just minutes the phone calls, text messages, and e-mails will take on a life of their own and spread like a wildfire. How easy and smart is that? The important thing is to have all that information at your fingertips, so you can effectively spread the word in a matter of minutes instead of hours or days. You can still distribute those missing-person posters or flyers. Later on you can forward the poster to the same people and ask that they distribute them around their community.

Next, call the police, if you haven't already, and be ready to provide them with *everything* they need to find your loved one. I emphasize the word everything. Your Individual Protection Packet with the Biographical Form will contain absolutely everything the police or detectives could possibly think of to initiate a successful search and rescue, and a thorough investigation. It will contain all the details and tools they will want and need.

With this Biographical Form you will now have not only dozens of names and telephone numbers, but you will have frequented *locations* at your fingertips. Search those locations you now know of and call family members and friends. Ask them to assist you by canvassing and searching those frequented locations.

You will know who your loved ones associate with and what vehicles they may be driving. You will be able to provide this information to the police on the spot, so they can instruct other police units to search specific areas and to issue a Be-On-The-Look-Out (BOLO) for other people and vehicles connected with your loved one.

You will have all the information and tools the police will need to start a successful search and rescue, a thorough and successful investigation. This detailed Individual Protection Packet and Biographical Form will act as a complete checklist not only for you, but for the police and investigators. In addition to the multiple photographs, names, locations, associations, and vehicles that may be involved, the police will have short video clips, fingerprints, DNA, medical records, and much, much more.

You will also discover how easily all this information can be carried with you everywhere you go; and for others to have and carry as well. Include your pets if you like. Take this information with you everywhere. It will all fit in your pocket or purse, or even on a key ring. Leave a copy at home and at work. Give a copy to a trusted relative, friend, or neighbor. Take it with you on a trip. It's like having a hip. It will always be at your side.

Why did I write this book? First, this is a very tragic and deadly problem for any family to face. Second, it is happening far too often in America. Third, there are many commercial products available that in reality are of little use alone. Some of these products are overpriced or a waste of money. Families and people need sound advice and fool-proof methods to protect themselves. You have it now.

Last, in many instances law enforcement authorities lack the manpower and resources to react quickly and efficiently to each and every missing-person report. Their call-outs and caseloads can be overwhelming. Their money and resources are limited, especially during this economic crisis where budgets are being seriously cut. This is especially true in smaller departments. These unfortunate shortcomings can and will lead to neglect or mistakes.

Crucial advice: There is no room for shortcuts or errors when it comes to finding your loved one. Do not delay and leave no stone unturned.

I priced this book to be affordable, so give a copy of this informative instructional guide as a gift to others you care about. You will understand by the end of this book how this can be a gift of love. I will in turn donate some of the proceeds from this book to various support organizations. See! Together we are fighting this national and deadly epidemic; and together we can encourage our government to do the same. I'll help you with that as well. Become an advocate for missing children and adults.

If you have your notebook and highlighter handy, let's get started.

Chapter 2

GENERAL INFORMATION

I'll provide a few examples of deadly predators later in the book, both adolescents and adults. These cases are disturbing, but important for you to know and to think about. It is time for all of us to pull the sheets from over our heads. Go ahead and look under the bed and inside the closet. I'll turn on the lights for you, but you have to do the hard part. Remember, knowledge and awareness is one of the keys to survival. The next step to personal security is prevention. Know what to do and how to do it. That is our goal—to stop an attack in the first place.

Thousands of children and young adults are kidnapped every year. "Family" abduction is the biggest culprit, but "non-family" and "stereotypical" abductions are numerous and very deadly situations. These are categories used by law enforcement. Sometimes a victim is not classified under any of these three groupings, because they voluntarily ran away with someone who they thought they could trust.

During conversations with the police there may be miscommunication that may very well result in the police downplaying the kidnapping, consequently affecting how they conduct their initial response. Sometimes they may be reluctant to even file a missing-person report. Sad, but true. You don't want that to happen. I'll explain more later.

The true number of runaways and kidnapped victims who are abused and exploited every year is staggering. Some people argue the facts and the numbers, even the police and prosecutors. Does it really matter if the person was kidnapped by force or trickery (manipulation)? There are thousands of cases where family members have kidnapped and abused or murdered their victims. Could they have run away, but were later held against their will? Does it matter if the number is in the hundreds or thousands every year?

No, what really matters is the extreme cruelty being inflicted upon each and every one of these victims. That must be stopped no matter what the cost and effort. It is inhumane for us not to pursue each case vigorously. Saving the life of a loved one here and now is more important and less costly than capturing terrorists around the world; and that effort has cost America trillions of dollars and unbelievable resources, to include the unnecessary loss of heroic lives. I'll elaborate on that later.

Know that the majority of these perverted predators will never allow a victim to leave their embrace, or to become a witness who will put them in prison—or back into prison. They will in all likelihood kill or try to kill their victim. That's another reality!

There are some extremely vicious, psychotic people in our society, both young and older. Again, they are real live monsters! You cannot hide under the sheets to escape them. You cannot simply lock your doors at night and think that makes you safe. You need better security. You need education and training. You need a plan.

You must be prepared to scare these predators away and know how to fight them off. Don't be naïve or defenseless. Don't become a victim. Be ready and be strong. It's not really that time-consuming or difficult to start taking real precautions and erect those security barriers. What usually precludes us from taking the necessary steps to protecting ourselves is that we can't be bothered. "*I don't know right now. I have too many other things to do.*" Really!

We often listen to these news reports and sometimes discuss these tragic stories during casual conversations, but most of us do not really listen or pay close enough attention. To us it is another world. Why aren't we listening and reacting? As I said, perhaps we think we are just too busy with more immediate matters. Perhaps we feel it is an unpleasant topic, so we refuse to think about it. Perhaps we have convinced ourselves—this will never happen to me. Maybe we think security is too expensive. It's not, and it is getting less and less expensive. I'll get you thinking and give you some inexpensive tips.

Let's look at the number of missing-person reports across our nation in another way. Okay, we said in any given year an estimated 990,000 missing-person reports will be filed. **That averages out to 2,700 missing persons a day.** Or, think about in this way. **Every 32 seconds a child or adult is reported missing.** Is this really happening in America? Every 32 seconds someone disappears!

Here is another way to look at these incredibly dreadful numbers—closer to home. That averages out to **19,800 incidents per state** or **866 per county every year**. That in turn averages out to 54 missing-person reports every day in your state or two people every day in your county. *Every day*, in the county in which you live, two people may disappear and some may vanish, never to be seen again. That's scary!

Are you still not convinced you or one of your loved ones can become a victim? Let's look at another serious issue often related to missing-persons and violent attacks: *forcible rape*. According to other studies and statistics, an estimated **683,000 women are "forcibly" raped every year.** Many involve kidnappings. That averages out to 1,871 forcible rapes every day. In America, one young girl or woman is forcibly raped every 1.3 minutes. Many other women are raped as a result of intimidation or coercion, and these rapes are not classified as forcible. Many rapes occur in a woman's own home, including college. Young boys and men are raped and kidnapped as well.

This is not only devastating to the victims and their families, but shameful for our great country. Where are our moral values—knowing right from wrong? Two answers: Many parents are no longer teaching responsibility and morals to our children because they are often too busy and or simply don't care. Amazing, but very true.

Second, today's morals and values are falsely portrayed on television, in the movies, and through the Internet. Even in the video games our children play. So, this is what our children learn and know: sex, violence, drugs, profanity, disrespect, etc. Our children are suffering from a lack of good parenting and are bombarded with a false sense of reality.

In November 2011, a five-year-old girl was playing outside a McDonald's in Ohio while her grandmother sat inside. A thirteen-year-old boy raped the little girl on the playground and video cameras at the restaurant aided in the boy's arrest. Three months later, the boy was sentenced to inpatient treatment and placed on probation. What made this thirteen-year-old boy commit such a crime?

Stop and think about all the horrible factors in this case. A thirteen-year-old commits rape. A five-year-old is forcibly raped. It happened at a McDonald's playground in broad daylight and with others around. There was no parental supervision? There are many more cases in which young children are raped, or gang-raped, by other adolescents. These are not isolated cases by any means. Somehow, the parents are responsible. What do you think? Whose fault is it when a child commits a dreadful crime?

I'm going to go off on a slight tangent. One most of us will recognize. How many times are children taken into custody by school officials and police where the parents adamantly place the blame on the teacher and the police? They won't necessarily blame their child and almost never themselves.

Here is one more story to illustrate this point. In November 2010, in a small town in Texas, an eleven-year-old girl was kidnapped and gang raped by at least eighteen to twenty boys and men ranging from ages fourteen to twenty-six. Many of them videotaped the assaults on their cell phones. Some people blamed the young girl and some blamed her mother. Some argued that the boys will have to live with this the rest of their lives, suggesting that was a punishment. Some argued the prosecution of the attackers was racially motivated. A writer for the New York Times wrote an insensitive article suggesting the girl was at fault and the editor of the NYT defended criticism against the reporter and the newspaper. What happened here?

I mention our missing-person and related problems here in America. Before I go any further, let me elaborate. I have lived and worked in numerous foreign countries (over twenty) and the same horrendous problem exists in every civilized and advanced nation. In third-world countries it is far, far worse. Anyone living or traveling throughout North America, Europe, Asia, North Africa, and any other region of the world needs to be just as careful—if not more. We are, in fact, fortunate to be living in this great country. But our government needs to do more, and it can do more; and, so can we as individuals and parents. I'll talk about that later—and how you can help.

Back to other crimes that may lead to missing person incidents and violent attacks. How much do you know about *date rape and date rape drugs?* Many young girls and women go on seemingly harmless dates and are forcibly raped. Usually the victim knows her assailant. Various drugs, including alcohol, are intentionally used by predators to rape women against their will. Two prescription drugs commonly used are GHB and Rohypnol, or "roofies." All it takes is a little pill in their drink. Alcohol alone is used as a date rape drug. Here is some personal advice to all young adults: "Everything in moderation." Especially when it comes to drinking alcohol.

Many young girls and women are semiconscious or totally unconscious during the rape. Some will not remember what happened once they wake up, but there will be tell-tale signs and possibly serious consequences later, to include pregnancy or sexually transmitted diseases (STD).

Young girls and woman do not need to be on an actual date with someone they know to be drugged and then raped or sexually abused. It could be a chance encounter with one of these monsters at a bar or nightclub. It could happen at a college party. It could even happen at a restaurant. As you leave the restaurant or club, feeling a little woozy, guess who is following you out the door? The stalker or the chance predator.

In July 2010, three men accosted a twenty-three year old woman in a Myrtle Beach, South Carolina bar, dragged her across the street by her arm, and raped her in their minivan. A fourth man later entered the minivan and raped the woman as well. This is just one of countless cases. Apparently she was too drunk to resist.

In April 2012, a female soldier from Fort Bragg, North Carolina left a bar with an employee who offered her a ride home. The man drove her home and that was the last time this twenty-three year old woman was seen. It turns out the man was a registered sex offender and was arrested, but only because he was not living where he was registered. The police supposedly claimed the employee was not a suspect. There were allegations of troubles between the female and her husband, but he was out of town that evening.

Many women who are unconscious when they are raped have no memory of it the next morning. Know that some rapists will take pictures of the victim in compromising poses as a trophy or to share with others. These devastating photos can even turn up on the Internet. Also know that some of the predators may return and, worse, develop an obsession.

This could be your wife, daughter, girlfriend, or sister. Somewhat surprisingly, many men and boys are kidnapped and are victims of rape as well.

Forcible and nonconsensual sex through the use of drugs or force occurs every minute of the day.

Visit **www.crimepreventiontips.org** and look at the Main Menu to learn more about college safety, date rape, self-defense, and other topics. There are other good websites. Awareness is all about research and learning. I'll include various websites in the back of the book. These sites are just to get you started.

Keep in mind, many kidnappings by casual acquaintances and strangers are often linked to sexual crimes. Sex is a powerful psychological inducement—as powerful and deadly as any drug. It can strip away a person's private inhibitions and moral principles, causing them to behave with a reckless disregard for their safety and the wellbeing of others. This can be true for both victim and aggressor.

Predators will take advantage of innocent people without hesitation or thought—and no matter what your condition or the circumstances. For these particular predators, sex alone is a controlling influence that causes them to act out in criminal behavior that may have serious or deadly consequences.

What about *violent crimes* in general? In addition to murder and forcible rape, there are other violent crimes to include assaults and robberies. Other studies and statistics show that well over **four million violent crimes are committed every year.** Four million! That averages out to over 11,000 violent attacks every day, or one violent attack every seven minutes. That averages out to 80,000 violent attacks in every state or 318 per county per year. Again, does that sound closer to home?

Here are some other statistics pertaining to children and teenagers alone: Over 102,000 children are missing and have never been found. That number is probably much higher considering *abandoned* children are not usually reported and probably become victims. How many children are abandoned? Estimates are from 5,000 to 15,000.

Another figure I read stated over one million children are the victims of child pornography, which is a *multibillion* dollar industry in America. Wait a minute! Child pornography in our country is a multibillion dollar business? Over 1.6 million children are sexually assaulted every year to some degree. Over 100,000 fugitive sex offenders cannot be found. Again, these are numbers that need not be argued or disputed. It is the absolute enormity of the problem we must recognize.

Folks, whatever the true statistics for any of these categories, these are alarming numbers and horrifying events. The numbers are *huge* and something must be done. The odds you or a loved one will be attacked or kidnapped are very high. Sadly our government is not doing enough; and frankly, neither are we as individuals and parents. Now you can. You will soon have the knowledge and the means.

There are several easy and simple steps you can take to protect yourself and your loved ones against these ill-fated odds and put your mind at ease. Why worry or suffer? As a parent who raised three children, I can tell you my wife and I constantly worried and still do. As a (retired) law enforcement officer and private security consultant, I am acutely aware of people and families who needlessly suffer at the hands of these savage animals and monsters.

You have taken a very important step by buying and reading this book. By learning what to do, you are on the right path towards a personal or family security plan. By developing a plan and actually doing something, you are on that path towards safety and security. Pat yourself on the back. You deserve it.

Keep in mind that when I talk about "personal security" I am including your "safety and security" at home, where you go to school, your place of work, or your favorite shopping area—any place you frequent or visit. These attacks can happen anywhere at any time.

This can also apply to driving in a car, or being a passenger on a plane or boat. *Carjackings* are another serious issue. Carjackers are violent criminals and have been known to kidnap drivers and occupants. The victims of carjacking have also disappeared or vanished! Violent *gangs* have been known to randomly attack people on the street. We all know that planes have been *hijacked* and even cruise ships and private boats are hijacked by modern-day pirates. These are all safety and security concerns.

Although airline hijackings seem to be a rare occurrence, we all recall the September 11, 2001, hijacking of four commercial planes involving 246 victims in one single day. There have been several other commercial airlines targeted since that horrific event. These airline attacks have taught us a valuable lesson: we cannot remain passive—we must fight back. The old philosophy was sit back and don't do anything to incite the kidnappers or terrorists. That security tactic didn't work, and it never will.

In 2010 alone, a total of fifty-three ships and boats were hijacked. Pirates captured 1,181 seafarers and killed eight of them. That number is increasing and the total over a period of years is also staggering. An average of 49,000 carjackings occur every year.

The bottom line: always exercise security and safety no matter where you are or what you are doing—even during your travels and vacations, especially international.

The next important step, after reading this book, is to actually do something. This is not a time to procrastinate and or cut corners. There are a lot of good suggestions and plentiful advice throughout this book. Are you using that highlighter or taking notes? Decide what you want to do and then do it. Do whatever is humanly possible.

Crucial advice: If a loved one suddenly turns up missing and you suspect foul play, even if it is just a "gut feeling" do not hesitate to call the police immediately. Then start your search using the Biographical Form.

I tell people to always trust their gut feeling. That is your internal survival instinct. It is that uncanny sense you get based on subconscious information you cannot explain to yourself or clearly articulate to others at that moment, but there are in fact reasons for your assumptions. It is like trying to remember a name. It is there, you just need to think harder! These gut feelings are your internal alarms going off. Your antennas are tingling. Some people might call it a sixth sense, but it is real. You can even learn to hone or enhance those inner feelings. Get in touch with your Zen. Or, just think harder.

What happens when you try to explain to the police why they should take action based on your vague report? Don't let denial or embarrassment hold you back from taking action. Don't listen when someone says you are being silly or irrational. Learn how to trust your survival instincts and, more importantly, to act upon them. Go with your gut feeling. Call the police! Call 911!

If you suspect foul play and decide to call the police first, while you are waiting for the police officer or detective to respond, start making those crucial phone calls right away. Send those text messages and e-mails with your loved one's description and photographs. Ask others to search various locations. When the police arrive, hand them a copy of your Individual Protection Packet and let them know what you have done. Brainstorming is a great tactic. We used to do it all the time during military missions, investigations and enforcement operations. Bouncing ideas off one another is smart. I hate when someone thinks they have all the answers.

With the valuable information provided in your Biographical Form, the police can start contacting and questioning everyone. The entire protection packet serves as a complete toolbox and thorough checklist for the police and investigators. The Biographical Form will enable the police to start making phone calls without wasting valuable time questioning you and collecting all this information. That alone takes hours. This form will help guide them through your daily activities and personal life—or the life of your loved one. It will give them valuable *investigative leads*. These leads are *clues* they need to follow up on ASAP.

CHAPTER 2: GENERAL INFORMATION

It is one thing when you call someone about your missing loved one, but it takes on a whole new meaning when a police officer or detective starts calling and questioning people. Some of your loved one's friends may be hesitant to talk to you, but they may not be willing to ignore or lie to the police.

Most police and investigators have a great deal of knowledge and experience in these matters. They can usually tell when someone is nervous or lying. Even over the telephone. They may know if someone on your list is a suspect or convicted criminal. They may know if certain predators and criminals frequent the same locations as your loved one. They can reach out for *informants/confidential sources*. The intelligence capabilities and resources available to law enforcement are usually extensive.

The names and all the other information in these protection packets are valuable insights that tell the police and detectives who to contact and where to look. These tools, such as DNA and fingerprints, will help the investigators determine if you or your loved one was in a particular location, for example a car, motel room, or house.

They can use certain information from your Biographical Form to *track and monitor* your loved one, such as a cell phone number, credit cards, or a license plate. By *pinging* your cell phone, they can narrow you down to a specific location—even a house, building, field, or moving car. In fact later, we will talk about the GPS features on a cell phone that will allow you to see where that phone is located.

By monitoring bank cards and credit cards they can see when and where they are used. Guess what comes with that ATM receipt? A video! Guess what is found in many businesses and even on street corners? Cameras! Along with discovering the exact date, time and location, they want to know who is on that video.

Here is a question that sounds simple, but that many people do not know. If a loved one turns up missing, who do you call? Don't say, Ghost Busters!

Do you call your city police department or the county sheriff's office? It could be the state police in rural areas.

Other than your local law enforcement, do you know who else you can contact? In addition to the local law enforcement authorities, there are other state and federal agencies you can contact, depending on the situation. Let's put those telephone numbers at your fingertips as well.

These other law enforcement agencies have the knowledge and expertise as it relates to interstate (cross-country) and international incidents involving missing persons. They employ experts who know how to locate missing persons and how to investigate complicated kidnappings. It is amazing what are professionals can achieve when they work together.

They can notify and alert authorities in other states and at our international borders, including air, land, and sea checkpoints as well as remote and secluded crossings. They can contact the proper authorities at our embassies and foreign law enforcement agencies around the world. Do you know about all the other agencies? You will now, and you may have to get personally involved. Sometimes you will have to make the phone calls and you will have to make things happen. I'll teach you how to prod them along.

The national missing-person and support organizations mentioned in this book provide excellent information on awareness and prevention. However, most important, they can assist you and law enforcement authorities with locating your loved one. Some of these quasi-governmental and private organizations will also provide you with moral and emotional support throughout this terrible ordeal. You won't be alone. Now you will know where to get professional advice and counseling.

Through this book you will learn not only about self-protection, but you will learn more about law enforcement and what it can do to help you. You will learn more about these support organizations that can assist you.

CHAPTER 2: GENERAL INFORMATION

This book is about knowledge, which is part of awareness. This book is about self-protection, which is part of prevention. These are the keys to survival.

Crucial advice: To dispel yet another myth, you do *not* need to wait twenty-four hours to report a missing child or adult. In fact, you don't have to wait any period of time. Call 911!

As I explained earlier, if a loved one is missing and you suspect foul play, contact your local police immediately. They must respond and take action. That initial conversation, again, may involve miscommunication that could result in reluctance by the responding police officer or detective to take this missing report seriously and to initiate an immediate search and rescue, or investigation. We will talk more about that throughout the book.

More crucial advice: If you or a loved one turns up missing you need a trained and experienced detective who specializes in missing persons.

A patrol officer is restricted and limited in what he can do. He will not have the required training and experience. You need a qualified *investigator* who has insight and all the resources available to him as a detective.

Once contacted, the police or a detective must respond and they must take an official report. That response needs to be in minutes—not hours. Once they take a report, there are certain internal procedures they must follow. It is rare nowadays that a police officer or detective will ignore internal policies and procedures, but it happens. You can't take that risk. Here is what you can do.

If you do not feel a police officer or detective is taking the report seriously or the necessary steps to find your loved one, then ask him about his "department policies and procedures" for a missing-person report. Big Question: Will an *Amber Alert* (children) or a *Silver Alert* (adults) be issued, and when? Believe it or not, Amber and Silver Alerts are not automatically initiated on all missing person reports. Why not? No doubt you will get an excuse.

If reasoning does not seem to be working, be *polite* and ask the officer for the name and telephone numbers of his "immediate supervisor." If that does not seem to work, demand to speak to next person in their "chain-of-command." Call the chief of police or the sheriff if you have to. Do not be timid or afraid to ask questions, and follow up on the police officer's response or the detective's investigation.

Learn what you can do to press the police into action and ensure a successful search and investigation. Learn how to get involved. You are not required to sit back and do nothing. It is your loved one who is missing. You may decide to contact other authorities or resources. That's your prerogative—your right.

The more help you and the police have, the better your chances of finding your loved one quickly and unharmed. Time is of the essence. You need to find them right away, within the hour or a few hours later. Having said that, you do need to trust and cooperate with the police. More on that point later.

What is *stalking*? There is a longer legal definition, but in short, *stalkers* are individuals (creeps) who are illegally harassing or following you, usually for a nefarious reason. What is one thing that all stalkers have in common? Psychosis (abnormal), meaning that their mental condition and their behavior is not rational or normal. What type and how extreme is their psychosis? Who knows? We just recognize it is not normal to secretly follow other people around or harass them. **It is estimated that over 1.4 million persons are stalked every year.** What! Over one million incidents a year?

Many of these monsters are living and stalking victims in your state, county, or city; in your neighborhood or right next door; at your school or place or work; where you shop or any other location you frequent or visit. Even

CHAPTER 2: GENERAL INFORMATION

the parks and playgrounds your children frequent are hunting grounds for these beasts. Movie theaters, sports arenas, and gyms can be trolling spots. Most states have very severe laws to prevent and punish stalkers. Why? Because more so than harassment, criminal stalking by predators usually results in violence or sexual assaults—to include murder.

Sex offenders and *pedophiles* are a serious problem in our country. Trust me when I say you do not want to bump into one of these monsters and attract their attention. Learn how to avoid them and learn what to do should you encounter one of these sexual predators. Learn now where these sex offenders live and keep your children away from their homes and haunts.

Yes, you can easily find their names and addresses near where you live. Enter your address and then check for a radius up to one mile or further. Do the same for any other location you frequent, e.g., your babysitter's address, daycare center, school, library, park, etc. If you know or suspect a sexual offender lives nearby, check them out on the *sexual offender registry* online. If you learn they are not living where they are registered, call the police and they may be arrested. Yes, you can make an anonymous call; just provide all the details, and make it easy for the officer or detective to investigate.

If you suspect someone may be a criminal or sexual deviant, contact the police and file an official report. Most law enforcement agencies have a good intelligence unit. Your information may be useful right at that moment or in the future. You may help the police catch a fugitive. If they are merely behaving inappropriately, get it on record and on file in the police computers. For the police and the courts it is all about "documentation" for future use.

Okay, how about an example. Some middle-aged creepy guy lives on your street by himself and he always has young kids coming to his house. Report it! Why? Because it just happened in my city. During television interviews after a local arrest, neighbors commented the single man living in their apartment complex seemed nice enough, but the comings and goings of young males made them feel uneasy. Their gut instincts turned out to be right, but they didn't *do* anything until it was too late. He was molesting the boys. Neighborhood situations of this nature can also involve drug trafficking and other crimes.

The neighbors should have reported their suspicions to law enforcement authorities earlier—not when interviewed by the media. Even if a crime had not been committed at the time, the matter could have been documented and investigated. Two or three complaints earlier on might have saved one or two victims.

Don't play detective with suspected neighbors and strangers. It will probably create a serious situation and you could get hurt. However, there is a way to learn more about suspicious people without exposing yourself. **Hire a private investigator.** There are PIs who specialize in personal security and there are PIs who specialize in missing-person cases. I'll talk more about that later. This is all part of awareness and prevention.

Other violent offenders include small or large groups of individuals committing violent attacks and other crimes. These groups include home invaders, street gangs, and organized crime.

Home invasions often happen for specific reasons; these hard-core criminals believe in exploding with violence to subdue people and force them into immediate submission. A home invasion usually involves a robbery, but can result in rape, beatings, and murders. It all starts with a knock on the door, or the offenders may storm through a front or back door left unlocked. *"Why did I open the door?" "Why did I leave my doors unlocked?"* Good questions!

Home invasions happen all the time and often involve the wrong house and the wrong people. The intruders, for some reason, thought the victims had drugs or money. An estimated **eight thousand home invasions occur every day** throughout our country. Yes, eight thousand every day! Again, many of them involve the wrong home.

CHAPTER 2: GENERAL INFORMATION

Home invaders may pose as law enforcement officers. The person knocking on your door may pose as a delivery person or a repairman while the others wait in the shadows. There are simple steps to help protect against a home invasion.

Unlike a surreptitious burglary (break-in), a home invasion is intended to be an overwhelming force of violence. In the military and law enforcement, we call it "shock and awe," also known as "rapid dominance." Any home can become a target. That is why home alarm systems and closed-circuit television (CCTV) camera systems are so valuable. Even the appearance of an alarm and cameras may protect you. Surrounding your house in lights is also important. It allows your neighbors and the police to see activity around your home. It allows you to look out and see them coming, and it makes it harder for them to walk up to your window or hide in shadows. Lights permit the bad guy to see the alarm warning signs and stickers, as well as the cameras.

Street gangs may also have a specific intent when it comes to violence and robberies, but they often attack with no apparent reason. Innocent people and families have been known to turn down the wrong street, where gangs swarm innocent strollers and vehicles. The victims are left for dead or are taken as a prize and for amusement. What happens to these victims while in captivity is sickening.

Gangs operate in major cities and can be found in smaller cities and towns. They are on the streets and in our schools. One report I read, said there are over **three hundred thousand gangs and eight hundred thousand gang members** across America. Wow! We have all heard of the Crips, Bloods, and Latin Kings. One of the more violent gangs spreading across America is the Mara Salvatrucha, commonly known as MS-13. Please go online and learn more about street gangs. Learn about all these threats.

Outlaw Motorcycle Gangs (OMG), especially the 1% (One Percenters), are considered both "criminal gangs" and "organized crime." Some of the more notorious OMGs you may recognize are the Hell's Angels, Outlaws,

Mongols, and Pagans. Many young girls and lawful motorcycle riders make the mistake of associating with these outlaw biker gangs, thinking it is cool. These groupies or wannabe bikers begin to hang out with the hard-core bikers. But these naïve souls are not being allowed to hang out—they are being drawn in. It usually turns out bad.

We also hear about *Organized Crime* such as the Italian, Russian, and Japanese mafias. They operate as larger families (crime syndicate) and smaller gangs. Cross any of their members and they may attack and kill without hesitation. These organized crime gangs also have their wannabes. Many people make the mistake of associating with organized crime figures, and the results are bad. Not a smart thing to do if you want a good future.

As I have repeatedly suggested, go online or to the library and research these various groups and gangs, especially if you live in an urban or inner-city environment. Research everything you are learning in this book. It helps you with your *situational awareness* and *preparedness*. Some people call it *street smarts*, or *common sense*.

Random killers and even serial killers have been known to act in pairs. You will read about some of these cold-blooded murderers further in the book. Even husband and wife teams have committed kidnappings, assaults, and murders. Most of the individual predators who thrive on the violence are deadly enough, but as a pair or small group they are simply overwhelming. Even a well-armed citizen is going to have a serious problem. One violent criminal or monster is bad enough, but in pairs and groups they are more difficult to fight off. To these gangs, violence is akin to a drug they must have.

Much like the sexual predators I described earlier, violent offenders are also controlled by their desires and lifestyles, or their environments. They find violence exciting and intoxicating. For gang members, an act of extreme violence or murder is a requirement—or a badge they wear. Once a group attack begins, it can become a vicious feeding frenzy. Like sharks or hyenas.

Through this book you will also learn how to protect yourself and your family from various *cybercrimes* that can result in violent and sexual attacks; and I'll discuss sexual content over the Internet. Discovering unidentified people online and then actually meeting with them can have deadly consequences.

Crucial advice: Never meet a stranger *alone*, no matter how interesting or appealing they may seem online or over the phone. Don't accept *rides* from strangers and don't *leave* establishments with strangers.

How can someone be violently attacked over the Internet? We already know criminals can lure you into an actual, face-to-face meeting. However, there have been numerous cases in which *Internet predators* have encouraged people to commit suicide by preying on their emotional and mental weaknesses. One man was recently convicted of persuading several victims to commit suicide. That was his sole motive and intent. Where did he find these victims? On suicide chat rooms and blogs. Did you know there was such a place on the Internet?

Suicide can also be the result of cruel and relentless *cyber-bullying*. There have been several cases where teenage girls were relentlessly harassed and bullied over the Internet. As a result, they committed suicide. What chat rooms and blogs do your children visit? Adults can be just as vulnerable.

You will even get advice on other cybercrimes to include *identity theft* and *computer hacking*. If a hacker steals your personal identity information, your bank accounts may be wiped out online before you know it. If they can't penetrate your online security, they will physically open bank accounts and obtain credit cards using your name and personal information. It takes victims months to years to fix the financial and many other problems associated with identity theft.

Cybercrime is already a huge threat and a rapidly growing danger, especially as it pertains to *cyber stalking* and *pornography*. There are ways to protect yourself and your loved ones from sophisticated Internet criminals and predators. Is the Internet bad? No! You just need to be aware of the threats over the Internet and avoid *temptations*. There are some excellent websites to learn more about cybercrimes and identity theft. Take the time to research all these topics. I'll provide some links in the back of the book and in various chapters.

Social networks such as Facebook, MySpace, Twitter, and online dating services are also hunting grounds for these violent offenders and sexual predators. Even Craigslist has become a hunting ground for these animals and monsters. They use these social networks, chat rooms, and blogs to lure you in, and once you are hooked, with the little information you reveal, they can draw you all the way in or come find you wherever you live.

Learn how to protect your children and teenagers from Internet predators and the many temptations. Learn how to protect every family member, adults as well. Even grandpa and grandma. Learn how to protect personal information over the Internet and on the telephone. Learn how to avoid traps and getting hooked.

Parents must wake up and realize the Internet is good, but it can be both a danger and a destructive temptation to your child or teenager. You must understand what these specific threats and temptations are and then monitor your children and teenagers' activities over the Internet. Again, the same can be said for many adults. The Internet is like a firearm. It can have a legitimate purpose or value, but you *must* take certain safety precautions. These precautions include education and prevention. They include rules and monitoring. Yes, I know you may trust your child, but you still need to be careful and diligent as a parent.

Think of it as like having a new driver's license and operating a motor vehicle on public streets. After walking out of DMV, would you give your teenage child unfettered access to a car and let them take off without any supervision or rules? Doesn't a driver's license require education and training to prevent accidents? The Internet is no different—only it doesn't require an age limit or permit, only a connection.

By the way, teenage vehicle deaths are another serious problem for parents to explore. The numbers are increasing. Motor vehicle crashes are the leading cause of death for teenagers. Those crashes often involve speeding, drinking and driving, and inattentive driving, including texting and talking on cell phones. Your child may be a passenger in a car driven by one of these irresponsible people. Teach them to say, stop doing that or let me out of the car.

Just for clarification, violent and sexual studies categorize an "adult" as anyone age eighteen years and older. This age distinction pertains to law enforcement and missing-person reports. I don't care what anyone says or thinks; teenagers are not adults fully capable of taking care of themselves. Not even at the age of eighteen or nineteen years.

When it comes to our protective laws, an eighteen and nineteen-year-old needs the same legal protections as a seventeen-year-old. This age limit must be changed to include all teenagers. If you decide to become a missing-person advocate, please address this particular point with your government officials and representatives. There are more government resources, efforts, and emphasis placed on finding missing children. Let's get those same resources for all our teenagers of any age.

Think about this. Some "adult privileges" begin at the ages of sixteen to nineteen years, but even then, a teenager is not an adult. Teenagers are given certain privileges to help them become responsible adults. It is a trial period. You can treat them like adults, as part of that growing-up process, but they should not be considered adults, especially by law enforcement and legal standards as it pertains to protecting our youth.

As long as they are your children, you are responsible for their behavior and wellbeing. Both! A part of love and responsibility is enforcing rules and making tough decisions. We have heard the term "tough love." Don't wait until after your children commit grave mistakes to consider a little tough love. You may be a little too late. I'll get off my parental soapbox now. But watch out. Later, I will get on my political soapbox.

Let's get back to the bad guys. While not always intelligent, and some are, most criminals and deviants can be very clever and cunning. With just a little bit of personal information to get them started, these criminals can find out more details and hunt you down in a matter of hours or days.

In fact, they may not need any information at all. If they have zeroed in on you, they might just follow you home or to other places. It's called physical surveillance—or stalking. Some of them are pretty good at this technique. During my career as an investigator, I have followed people by myself, for days and weeks, and they never had a clue I was watching their every move. That includes following them in a car and into buildings. As the professionals say, check your six o'clock. (That means your behind.) More on that coming up. Not your behind—criminal stalking and surveillance.

The more calculating predator will begin learning more about you or a family member. Through the Internet they can now look at detailed pictures and images of you, your neighborhood, your home, and where you go to school or work. Depending on how current the satellite and street views, they may even see a picture of your car parked in the driveway. They can see a detailed picture of your home and your property layout, as well as the surrounding properties and neighborhood. They can find out what homes are for sale or empty, and what streets lead in and out of your development.

Using the Internet, predators can also perform *background checks*, or *record checks*. They will quickly learn details of your personal life, as well as that of each of your family members. These checks are gleaned from *open source* records (government and public) through commercial databases, which will include official government records you assume are confidential or protected. They are not. Once predators have located the source of the records, they can go to courthouses and other government facilities to obtain "original" documents containing even more details—some very personal or intimate.

With a little more physical surveillance they will be able to formulate a sinister plan that can turn deadly. Of course you can be the victim of a random attack or one that is less sophisticated. This book will help you learn how to impede or block such efforts, both calculated and spontaneous. Find out how you can scare them away by becoming a *hard target* as opposed to a *soft target*. Make yourself a hard target, no matter where you are.

Not all missing-person incidents are sinister. Children and adults turn up missing for several reasons. Sometimes we just forget to call and let someone know where we are. This needs to become a hard and fast rule at home. Make a phone call! Send a text. Many times there is just a miscommunication between parents; or with schools and care givers. Always double check your efforts.

If you can't reach your child or loved one by telephone then call the school, neighbors, or your loved one's close friends. Do you know who their close friends are and their telephone numbers? Do you know the parents of their close friends? Do you know whom they associate with in the neighborhood? You don't! Find out and include this information in the **Biographical Form**. Include a description and license plate number of vehicles you know they use for transportation, especially if it is a close friend or a boyfriend or girlfriend. The Biographical Form is going to be the crux of your new security plan.

Missing incidents can also involve an accident of any kind, in which the victim of that accident cannot contact someone right away. Perhaps they are unconscious or unable to communicate. Sometimes the police and emergency rescue cannot figure out whom to call. Everyone should have an **"Emergency Identification Card"** in their possession. You are going to learn how to make one. I dedicated a Chapter to that valuable tool.

Crucial advice: Family members and friends need to make quick phone calls, or send text messages, and keep in touch with one another. This includes children, teenagers, spouses, and parents. Include details of where you are, who you are with, and where you are going.

Parents, if you establish this rule, do not turn those phone calls into the "Twenty-One Questions" game, or an interrogation. Okay! Be thankful they are calling you and keeping you informed. If you convince them to start calling, just bite down on your finger, except to take it out at the end and say, "Thank you." Then stick your finger back in your mouth.

But, don't stick that finger in your ear. Listen to what they are telling you and write it down if necessary. Locations and times are very important to the police. Remember those ATM videos. Many businesses and public areas have security cameras as well. If something happens, there are witnesses to be located and interviewed. The police need to know where and when a victim was in a certain area. It's all in the details!

In most every event, either a family abduction or a kidnapping by a stranger, the incident is going to cause a great deal of emotional and mental trauma that may take years for a victim to overcome. We may not recognize or understand the extent of their emotional trauma and suffering, but the victim of a kidnapping will always need professional counseling afterwards. Always!

If you are a victim of a kidnapping or physical assault, don't try to suck it up and be tough. Don't be embarrassed or keep it a secret. Always seek medical assistance for both physical and mental injuries. Always report a crime to the police and help get that menace off the streets before he attacks another person.

This includes victims of rape and other sexual abuse, no matter what the circumstances. If you are the victim of *nonconsensual sex*, meaning you did not have sex willingly, then contact the authorities and seek medical attention immediately.

A victim of a sex crime will need both medical attention and professional counseling. There is no reason to feel ashamed or embarrassed. Again, don't keep it a secret. Don't let the perpetrator, if it is someone you know, trivialize the matter or intimidate you into keeping your mouth closed. Tell someone you love and tell the police, so they can see to it this person does not harm someone else. Let's get that predator off the streets and away from other innocent people. If it is not a habitual predator, then perhaps that person can be taught a valuable lesson. If you are a victim you are not at fault. You are innocent and they are guilty.

Let's talk some more about reports and investigations. It makes my blood boil when I notice how sloppy and lazy some police officers and investigators can be. Not many, but a few. There is no excuse for even one poor investigator in a department or agency when lives are at stake. I have seen sloppiness and laziness countless times. Yes, we have our bad apples just like any other profession, but I will say that most police officers and investigators are true professionals you can trust.

Our law enforcement departments and officers are not always infallible. They make mistakes just like in any other profession. They are professionals, but they have their good days and their bad days just like anyone else. A good officer can have a bad day when he or she is distracted by problems at home. Law enforcement officers are human too, and they can lose their professional demeanor at times. You try fighting and arguing with a bunch of criminals all day while going through a divorce or bankruptcy.

If a uniformed police officer arrives on the scene, give him your entire Individual Protection Packet, including the Biographical form, and then ask for a detective. If you are told there is not a detective available, find out if your case will be assigned to a trained investigator and how quickly. That detective needs to respond to the scene in less than an hour.

Some patrol officers are allowed to conduct *preliminary* investigations, but they do not have the time, resources, training, or experience to conduct a proper and thorough investigation. Not to mention a missing person investigation is top priority. If necessary, get on the phone with the department supervisors and go through that chain of command as previously mentioned. Did you highlight that part?

I'll say it again: you have only a few hours to find your loved one before the odds turn against you. You cannot afford any delays or mistakes. Yes, some cases might seem routine at first, but you cannot afford the mistake of thinking about them that way. Later in this book you are going to learn law enforcement terms and what they mean. It will help you understand their unique jargon and structure.

Crucial advice: There is nothing routine about any missing-person report. Assumptions are dangerous. Remember, you want to find them as quickly as possible, before they are harmed or vanish.

It is important for *you* to be involved in an investigative case, and it is important for you to know how to coordinate and communicate with law enforcement, as well as with the prosecutors. Once a case goes to trial, dealing with the prosecutor will be a whole new experience. It can be a good experience, or it may require more struggles. Many prosecutors have struck *plea bargains* with a defendant and his attorney without discussing this with the victim or the family. That should never happen. The prosecutor's office represents your rights, not just the law.

In most states, it is the District Attorney (DA) and Assistant District Attorneys (ADA) who prosecute crimes and civil violations. At the federal level it is the US Attorney and Assistant US Attorneys (AUSA). The Attorney General (AG) exist at both levels and oversees all offices. That is the chain of command.

The law enforcement authorities are the experts, so try to trust them and let them do their job. However, I have learned not to always take everyone's word as gospel or to place my life in other people's hands: not the police or lawyers, not even my doctor or accountant. You need to know what is going on and have a good grasp on the situation. However, you should be just as rational and calm towards the police as they are towards you. It's important for your loved one! Work with the police and investigators. Most everything in life is a two-way street.

Crucial advice: This is yet another myth to be dispelled. The crucial time period in which to locate a missing person is said, by some so-called experts, to be the first twenty-four, forty-eight, or seventy-two hours. This is absolutely incorrect. The crucial time period in which to locate a missing person is mere hours.

Make sure you point that out to the police officer or detective. Think about it. How fast can a person be transported to another county, state, or even a foreign country? That usually depends on where you live, but that's right: it can be done in hours, not days. As explained, this is a traumatic event for any person—child, teenager, or adult. They need to be rescued as fast as possible.

How fast would you want to be found if you were missing due to a kidnapping? How long could you tolerate being bound, gagged, beaten, or sexually assaulted? How long would you want to be trapped in a wrecked car or lying in a strange hospital bed alone? Right, you would want to be found and rescued right away. Get these Individual Protection Packets, including my Biographical Form, completed and implement some of the additional security and safety precautions that will be discussed in this book. I'll give you plenty to think about.

In some instances your protection packet may contain crucial information and investigative leads the police and detectives may unfortunately overlook until the next day, or even days later. This happens a lot. Don't let this happen! Again, the Biographical Form serves as a *checklist* for investigators. Trust me. They will love it.

The rest of the Individual Protection Packet gives the police and investigators the tools they need to act fast, i.e., proper photographs, two video clips, voice print, fingerprints, DNA, medical records, etc. I read once that a professional detective claimed DNA was not important in a missing-person case. Incredible! Fingerprints and DNA will help law enforcement officers determine if your child or loved one was in a particular vehicle, motel, house, field, or in some other location.

DNA may be found on a suspect where there is no other evidence. These DNA leads can keep detectives and prosecutors headed in the right direction and win a prosecution. Many offenders have been arrested and then let loose due to a lack of evidence or proof.

How hard is it to produce these protection files on each family member? Not hard. Just follow the step-by-step instructions in this book. All you need is a digital camera, computer, scanner, USB flash drive (thumb drive), and a few other items you can purchase at a local pharmacy or online. There will be alternatives and choices for you to make. If you do not have everything you need, then borrow the items or get someone to help you. No more excuses.

Back to the bad guys. What kind of monster brutally and savagely harms an innocent person? The answer is a very evil and mentally deranged individual. I have personally met some of these monsters, and I know what they are capable of doing to another human being. I have talked to them and looked them in the eye. Some of them have absolutely no remorse and when they do, they are most likely pretending.

Many defense attorneys are responsible for convincing judges to let their monster go free. I do not understand how these attorneys and judges live with themselves. They say it is about the legal system and the defendant's rights—even when the defendant is convicted of an exceptionally brutal and heinous crime. Wrong! When the crime involves vicious brutality against an innocent person, especially cold-blooded murder, then it is about the rights of the victim and the families. It is about justice and protecting society.

CHAPTER 2: GENERAL INFORMATION

If you are a member of a group or organization involved in field trips or vacations, I included an abbreviated version of the Individual Protection Packet and Biographical Form. You will have to decide what information to collect. But do something. Don't assume nothing bad will happen when someone is entrusted into your care and protection. We all know Murphy's Law, "If anything can go wrong, it will." I am a religious man, but I do not subscribe to the belief that everything is in God's hand or His plan. It is not.

Please read the **Annual Report filed by the National Center for Missing and Exploited Children** (NCMEC). Go to the NCMEC website at www.missingkids.com and download this informative report. If you browse only one website on missing persons, please take the time to research this site carefully. It offers great publications for children and adults. It also offers "**NetSmartz**," an interactive computer game to help teach your children and teenagers about personal safety. Get started today.

Visit www.klaaskids.org and learn more about the **Klaas Kids Foundation**. Visit www.pollyklass.org and learn more about the **Polly Klaas Foundation**. The names are similar, but they are two separate organizations. They can both provide you with immediate help and valuable training material and resources for protecting children. There are many other organizations to learn about. Do your research.

Order some books and videos for your younger children and teenagers today. Review them before you sit down with your children and review some of the websites I have mentioned first, then go over this material with your children. Give them the books and videos to watch again later on their own. Less pressure and a little privacy goes a long way with children and teenagers. This is a continuing process. Learning and training never ends.

Let's learn some more information. After all, this book is meant to make you start thinking. As you read in the introduction, children and adults turn up missing every second of the day. Family abductions and violent kidnappings happen every minute of the day. People are violently attacked and sexually assaulted every minute of the day. People disappear as the result of accidents or simply run away from home every day. It is naïve and irresponsible to think it cannot happen to you or your loved ones.

Awareness and prevention are the keys to *personal security* and *survival*. Included in this book are easy-to-follow instructions for completing personalized protection packets for yourself and each of your loved ones. Your personalized Individual Protection Packets and Biographical Forms are a crucial part of your overall personal and family *security plan*. Don't wait; get them done now.

Anyone who is successful in business and life has a plan and sets goals (milestones) to measure their success along the way. Military, law enforcement, and security professionals are mission oriented and trained both to succeed and to survive. They know you need a plan to prevail. Do you have a security plan for you and your family? Well, you will soon. Congratulations on taking the first step by buying this book. The second step of your plan is preparing the protection packets. The third step is learning more.

Knowledge is a part of awareness and prevention. Knowledge is not only power—it is strength. Know what threats are out there. Know what to do and how to fight back. Understand why you need to find your loved one in a few hours and know how to find them as quickly as possible. Know what specific steps you need to take and whom to contact.

This is something you may stumble upon. While researching this book I found an older website on which the producer(s) tried to debunk the problem of missing children and adults. I found various news articles as well. They claimed information and statistics were purposely manipulated and distorted to make the problem appear worse than it really is and to create an unnecessary hysteria. Hysteria! You will read most of these statistics and realize that they come from various crime reporting procedures set forth by the Department of Justice (DOJ) and the Federal Bureau of Investigation (FBI). This is a very real and serious problem.

CHAPTER 2: GENERAL INFORMATION

There are always the naysayers and conspiracy theorists. They refute anything and everything. People tend to argue and get hung up on statistics and numbers. The exact figures and numbers mentioned in this book are not important. They were found on the Internet through government reports and studies in the private sector. Don't try to dissect or deny these figures and numbers.

This book is not a research paper; it is an informational paper and a step-by-step guide. If someone wants to argue about any facts or numbers in this book, tell them to go bark up some other tree. If they disagree with what are legitimate opinions and advice—fine. Then ask them for a better idea or solution. Maybe they will have something positive to offer.

This book is intended to give you informative insight so you can make sound decisions. The statistics and numbers in this book are provided to help you understand and recognize the sheer magnitude and gravity of this growing and lurking danger. The odds are against you…they are against us. We can't count on the government and police alone. We can't count on our schools or businesses to provide the proper security we need to survive and go unharmed. We must rely on ourselves.

If you want absolute proof of what you are reading, you are encouraged to do your own research. This is my professional advice as a thirty-nine-year veteran regarding any matter. Do your own research on all of these topics. There are dozens of websites and books to help you learn more. I provide references at the end of the book. When you finish this book, don't put it away. Get to work. You should start by researching all the links provided in the back. Spend an hour or two on each website.

I could provide hundreds of heartbreaking stories, but they are there for the finding. There are many cases, but here are just three to illustrate the point about younger psychotic murderers:

A mother was shopping with her two-year-old child. Two ten-year-old boys lured the child away from his mother and kidnapped him. They walked this toddler to a secluded area far away from the shopping center, where they brutally tortured and sexually molested the child before beating him to death. At least thirty-eight witnesses recalled seeing the two older boys walking hand in hand with the crying toddler and occasionally stopping to strike the poor child or knock him down to the ground. Their excuse for not intervening was, "*They didn't think anything of it.*" Wow! They weren't seeing the potential problem— the threat. No one made the effort or took the time to intervene. Sad! Very sad!

Another thirteen-year-old burglarized a neighbor's home and brutally stabbed a twenty-seven-year-old woman, who fortunately survived. Unfortunately, the crime was not solved. Two years later, that same boy, now age fifteen, attacked again and this time viciously killed three neighbors in their seemingly safe home: a mother and her two daughters. He was convicted of murder as a minor. A minor! Twenty years later, a guard was stabbed by this inmate during a prison fight. This monster is eligible for release in the year 2020. He too will be back. Why? Who is his next victim?

A thirteen-year-old kidnapped a four-year-old boy and savagely tortured and sexually assaulted the child before committing cold-blooded murder. Even though this young teenage assailant was tried and convicted as an adult, he is eligible for parole. He will be back.

Why does a juvenile who commits torture, sexual assault, and cold-blooded murder get a second chance after being convicted? Do the children and families get a second chance? What about the next victim and their family? None of these cases were unfortunate accidents. They involved cold-blooded murder and unimaginable cruelty.

Later in this book you will read more stories involving adult murderers and serial killers. Many of them are arrested and convicted of heinous crimes and released back into society as well. Not just a few—a lot! Aside from the issue of age, why does our judicial system allow psychotic torturers and killers back into society, where they most always attack and murder again? I'll talk more about *criminal recidivism* (repeat offenders) later.

Keep in mind that the three cases described above were to demonstrate that these animals and monsters are adolescents as well, seemingly innocent youngsters who may be playing with your children. The adult animals and monsters come in far larger numbers and are more powerful—more cunning. Learn how to protect yourself and your loved ones. We are vulnerable at any age by any age.

Lt. Col. Dave Grossman, a bestselling author, has written a number of books. Look at his article on, "Are We Conditioning Our Children to Murder." Visit: http://www.killology.com/article_trainedtokill.htm. This is another topic you may want to explore. Later in the book, I will talk about violent games and movies.

Here is a good example of education and fighting back. In February 2012, a video on television (and YouTube) showed a twenty-five-year-old man snatching up a small girl in his arms at a Walmart store in a small town near Atlanta, Georgia. Her mother was a few aisles over buying groceries. The seven-year-old girl started kicking and screaming until the man sat her back down and fled the store. Security cameras tracked the man to the parking lot and a description of his car was also obtained. Within an hour police had Thomas Woods in custody. The little girl said she remembered her training about "*stranger danger*." She fought back and she attracted attention. She is now alive and unharmed. Awesome!

By the way, Thomas Woods had been recently released from prison where he served seven years for murdering a relative when he was seventeen years of age. Woods shot his uncle in the head and then robbed him before burying his body in the backyard. How did police find Woods after he murdered his uncle and fled the area? Police tracked the credit cards and cell phone Woods took from his uncle. Most criminals are stupid and make mistakes that can help us.

Why was Woods charged with manslaughter and released after only seven years? Because of a legal technicality. Two months later, after the attempted kidnapping of this little girl, prosecutors were racing against the clock to indict Woods, so he would not be released from jail on bond. If Woods is convicted and sentenced, will he be released again to attack another innocent person? Probably! Has he violently and sexually assaulted other children and adults authorities don't know about? It's likely. Remember all this for later.

In 2012, a 10-year-old girl and her two-year-old brother were walking down a Philadelphia street after buying candy a neighborhood store. A man suddenly came up from behind and tried to snatch the little girl. She fought back and the boy screamed. Because they fought back, the man dropped the girl and fled. Local street and business cameras caught the incident on tape. These private videos and the social media have been used in numerous cases to solve murders, rapes, kidnappings, etc. In fact, the Philadelphia Police Department has been a pioneer in the use of YouTube and social media, including Twitter and Facebook, to help solve crimes. Does your local police department use these crime solving methods? Ask them.

Think about this. Do you buckle your seat belt before you ride in a vehicle? Do you lock your doors and windows at night before going to bed? Do you wear a life preserver when you go boating, or put on a safety vest when you go jogging or hunting? Most people already have alarm systems for the home and car. These are basic security precautions we have learned about and hopefully use. But we can learn more.

Everyone should have both these alarm systems. However, did you know the big alarm signs in the front and back yard scares predators away before the alarm sounds? That makes sense, doesn't it? Just seeing that big sign and those bright stickers on the doors and windows lets the bad guy know there is an alarm system that will wake you up and notify the police. Hopefully he will leave you alone and go find another house or person. Good for you—bad for the other person. They should have bought an alarm, or this book.

There are a lot of little things we do to protect ourselves, but there are always more and better steps we can take for real protection. Learn what they are and start practicing (training) a good security plan. I'll help you with that. The hard part will be teaching this to your children. Of course children happily listen to everything we tell them. Ha! However, as I mentioned earlier, there are some good books and videos you can purchase that are designed and written specifically for younger children and teenagers. There is information on the Internet. Have older teenagers and adults read this book. This includes grandparents. We are never too old to learn.

In addition to local and state programs for missing children and adults, there are national-level programs and organizations that are funded in whole or in part by the federal government. These quasi-governmental organizations at the federal and state levels are usually dependent upon volunteers and donations.

Research and then reach out to these national and state organizations. Give them a call now and learn more about their responsibilities and services. Pledge your support as well and help them help all of us. Write down their emergency contact information and program (store) these numbers in your home telephone and cell phone. If something happens, call them immediately.

Four of these national support organizations you need to learn about include the **National Center for Missing and Exploited Children (NCMEC)** and **Let's Bring Them Home (LBTH)**.

Two others are the **National Center for Elderly Abuse (NCEA)** and the **International Center for Missing and Exploited Children (ICMEC)**.

Why NCEA? Because *elderly abuse* is an important topic and can be linked to missing adults. Also know there are international support organizations. NCMEC works with ICMEC. I also like the Polly Klaas foundations. There are two of them. Contact information for various organizations will be provided at the end of this book.

Right here in my town we have the **Global Child Rescue of North Carolina** (GCR-NC). You probably have a GCR in your state, or a similar organization. Many volunteers work hard to protect all of us. Find out who they are and offer your support. Keep in mind there are other organizations. I'm just pointing out a few. Google the terms, "*organizations for missing persons*" and "*international organizations for missing persons.*" You can also substitute the words adults and children for persons. Spend a few hours browsing and reading. Again, don't forget to use your notebook and pen. Then make those phone calls.

Because of funding issues, some organizations close down or merge with other organizations, so you need to stay current on your research. There are also private organizations you will read about over the Internet that are really not equipped to help you as much as the organizations listed above. You do the research and you decide.

Some of the organizations you may learn about may sound like organizations, but can instead be *private investigators* or other private organizations that specialize in missing-children cases. They may be able to help you as well. Maybe not. Explore all possibilities. I'll explain more about PIs in another chapter.

When you call someone, ask them detailed questions about their organization. First question: "How long have you been in existence?" Second, "How do you receive funding?" (government or private donations?). Third, "How many people do you employ, including both paid workers and volunteers?" Fourth, "What are your government certifications?" (Does the federal or state government oversee or monitor your operation in any manner?) These are just starter questions. Ask as many questions as they will answer. Your first goal is to determine if this is a legitimate organization. The next two goals are to determine if they can help you now and exactly how they can help you should a loved one disappear or vanish.

Crucial advice: As you learn more about these law enforcement agencies and support organizations, decide which ones you want to program into your home telephone directory and your cellular telephone. Program these important numbers into your children's cell phones as well.

As far as **calling 911** from home or your cell phone, please make sure every child in your home knows how to call 911 in the event of any emergency. There have been several wonderful stories where very young children had the knowledge and ability to call 911 in an emergency. Don't worry about the child's communication capabilities; the emergency dispatcher will understand who is on the other end of the phone, figure out the problem, and know where to send the emergency responders.

Sit down and discuss this particular topic with your children. Conduct a few rehearsals. They do not have to actually dial the number, but see if they are capable of picking up the telephone receiver. Pretend dialing the number and have them tell the pretend dispatcher they need help. Of course you will stress to your child the seriousness of calling 911. Go on the Internet and Google "*teach children how to call 911.*" There are several websites with a lot of good information.

We all know about calling 911 in the event of an emergency, but you also need to know **nonemergency telephone numbers**. These numbers need to be programmed in your home telephone directory and your cell phone contacts list. These numbers can include the city police department, the sheriff's office, and your state or highway police. You can include special sections that deal specifically with missing persons. Why? Thanks for asking!

Calling 911 on a cell phone might be tricky. It won't necessarily be, but it is a problem in some states and areas. In fact, over half the calls made to 911 are now made over cell phones, so the government is trying to fix various issues.

I recently read in a magazine that in most locations you can now dial **112** from a cell phone in an emergency. I called it from my cell phone and someone did answer. But, he told me to call 911 from my cell phone—not 112. See what you learn when you actually *do* something. Try it in your area.

Many people use cell phone in different areas and states when they travel, including international.

When I was in northern Maine, my cellular calls sometimes jumped over the border to Canadian towers. Hey! At one time 911 calls made from a cell phone were directed to the state police, but now they are usually directed to the local police or emergency services in the area from where you are calling. Again, those issues are being worked on, but they may not be resolved in your area.

Let's go with another example. You are away from home and you receive a frantic phone call from your older child who has been (a) seriously hurt, (b) someone is following them, or (c) someone is trying to break into the house. Where are they? What exactly is happening? Do you have time to start with the Twenty-One Questions? No! Tell them to hang up and call 911. Now what do you do as thoughts race through your head during your panic attack?

You can call the police as well. Who do you call? If you dial 911 you will get the police or emergency services in your current location. This is why you need to have nonemergency numbers stored in your cell phone. You don't have time to call 411 for information. Now you can call the Hometown Police Department and tell them what is going on. Ask them for help.

Another option is to call one or more neighbors. Do you have their numbers programmed on your cell phone? Are they listed on your

CHAPTER 2: GENERAL INFORMATION

Biographical Form? Of course you can call friends and relatives as well, but a neighbor is on the scene.

We all know that emergency dispatchers have caller ID and know who is calling and from where. How do cell phones work? Nowadays, some cell phone calls to 911 automatically triangulate off three nearby cell towers to identify your location. Some cell phones have a built-in GPS device that triangulates off cell towers and satellites in outer space. GPS stands for Global Positioning System. Amazing stuff!

The moment you call 911, your location is determined, and this is how your call is directed to the nearest dispatcher. Even if you don't know where you are, the dispatcher might. Some people say, *"I don't like Big Brother watching my every move"* Okay! If you have something to hide—fine. There will be more on the lifesaving GPS later.

In addition to owning a cell phone and personal GPS devices, I would strongly advise you take a look at getting **OnStar** for your vehicle. Foolproof communication is critical to survival. OnStar provides emergency assistance, navigation, and communication connectivity when you are away from home. If you are lost or in trouble you simply push a button and call for information or assistance. No searching for and dialing numbers. No worrying about cell phone coverage and dead batteries. It is your personal 911.

OnStar will be able to see exactly where you are located, and its advisors are prepared to handle different emergencies. If someone is attempting to attack your car or following you, call OnStar with the push of a button. If you are locked out of your car, they can unlock your door. If you are lost, they can tell you where you are and give you directions. Broke down? They can order up some roadside assistance. They can even locate your car if it is stolen. If you have an accident, the system will automatically summon the police. Right, OnStar can sometimes recognize you just had an accident, and if you are unconscious help will be on the way. Wow! OnStar is your personal guardian angel. Go online and research this valuable lifesaving tool.

Some states may have a different number for 911 when using a cell phone, such as 611 or #77. I already told you about the new 112 number. That didn't work for *me*. Well, in a way it did. I got some dispatcher somewhere. This is something you should research for your area and state, and for other areas you visit. Know which number to call from your city and county, as well as from your home or place of work or school, when using either your land line or your cell phone. Always be prepared! Training and rehearsals are important steps in being prepared.

Your cell phone provider can probably answer your questions. Also call your local police department and state police to ask about calling 911 on a cell phone. You can even call 911 (and 112) and tell them you are testing your cellular telephone coverage, and they will understand. Just don't call them too many times in one day, and don't try to order a pizza. They take all calls seriously.

Make a test call from your home and, as an example, try calling from your child's school or your place of work. Always be prepared! Always test out your ideas and rehearse them with your entire family. Training and mental rehearsals work. We do this in military and law enforcement agencies all the time. What is a *mental rehearsal?* That is where you imagine a mission (task) or problem and then mentally walk your way through that task or problem step by step. In your mind you can throw in the "what if" situations. Just do this over and over and visualize every detail in your mind. It is amazing how much you will predict and remember.

Crucial advice: Take the time to discuss a security plan with your entire family. Train and conduct mental rehearsals. Turn it into a fun game for your children.

Some departments can be tricky when you call and ask for these numbers. If you call and ask for a seven-digit number in the event of an emergency, they might tell you to call 911. Tell them you understand this, but you want a twenty-four-hour, seven-digit emergency number just in case. If they

CHAPTER 2: GENERAL INFORMATION

are not being cooperative, simply ask them for their "twenty-four-hour, nonemergency number to a live person." People can be difficult at times.

If you have an actual missing-person case and a police officer or detective has been assigned to your case, ask them for the main number to their office and the direct number to their desk. Also ask them for their cell number. Do they have a partner you can call? Police officers get sick and go on vacations. Who will you talk to if they are not available? Then, program these numbers into your home telephone and your cell phone—both for the detective and his partner. You may even want their supervisor's name and numbers.

When you have critical information to pass along, the last thing you need is to have a hard time reaching the appropriate person. Same thing with any of these national support organizations; if you have a personal point-of-contact, program their direct numbers as well. Things tend to work better when personalized, or when one person has all the information and details.

I can't say enough about the **National Center for Missing and Exploited Children** (NCMEC). The services it provides to all of us are absolutely incredible. The same can be said for its website. There is so much to learn from this one organization and on this one website alone. When you have conducted your own research, then research NCMEC's website along with your children, so they can learn as well. By conducting your own initial research, you will be better prepared to help your children navigate the website and services.

Show them the "**NetSmartz**" program (game) and get them started on this fun way to learn. This is a valuable tool for teaching your children what they need to know. You can also take a look at the **Child Victim Identification Program** (CVIP) and the **Cyber Tipline** to report and learn about child pornography and other threats.

PLEASE, sit down and explore everything NCMEC has to offer on this website. Then call a representative and talk to them. Again, always ask a lot of questions and always take good notes. You should be writing down information, to include names and telephone numbers. Ask how you can learn more, and consider becoming a volunteer or donating to this wonderful organization.

Here is some good advice on **organizing information and notes**. This is not about personal security; it's just free advice at this point. (You already bought the book.) My wife and I keep a notebook (journal) by the telephone. It is actually a thick multiple-subject notebook you buy for school. When we talk to anyone, we always write down (in this order) the date (mm/dd/yy), the company or business, the person's name, and all their contact information. Then we write down some key notes. This journal is a great method for keeping track of all the things we need to know and find at a later date. I usually highlight the company or person's name in the event I need to find the information later. I use yellow and she uses pink. She is such a girl.

Back to the question of more government protection. Am I jumping all around? Okay, but I told you I'm not a professional writer. I'm just full of good stuff. Ha! Government funding for missing-persons programs and advanced systems and networks is totally inadequate and unacceptable. Our federal and state governments together spend over a *trillion dollars* ($1,000,000,000,000) a year on programs and projects that have absolutely nothing to do with public security and protection. How much does the government spend on public security and protection here at home? It is a drop in the bucket.

The federal government has a constitutional [legal] mandate to protect its citizens both at home and abroad. State governments have a similar [state] constitution and mandate as well. Our government was designed to protect us. If our government officials and representatives tell you that providing security and protection to its citizens, as a whole, is not a legal mandate then they should not be in office. It is also a moral obligation. Elected and appointed officials take an oath to uphold and defend the US Constitution. It is ordered in the Constitution that the government will protect its citizens. It starts with, "We the People" A known police motto is "To serve and protect," right?

Law enforcement and police typically have a reactive role, and over the years they have learned the value of implementing proactive measures. However, as a nation, we need better proactive measures with new and better reactive initiatives as they pertain to an innovated national missing-persons program. As a country we in fact have the money and technology. If you are told there is not enough money, then someone is blowing smoke up your wazoo.

In comparison to the billions of dollars wasted on foolish projects very little money is spent on a national missing-persons program that truly help us protect our children through awareness and prevention. Very little is spent to help law enforcement locate our loved ones as expeditiously and efficiently as possible in order to save their lives. Even today, some police officers and investigators will downplay a missing-person report to save time, effort, and money. It is not necessarily the officer or detective's fault or intention; however, most departments across the country have become slaves to internal budgets and policies.

NCMEC and LBTH are a good start for a national program, but even these private organizations need more funding and more resources. Why do they need to rely on donations along with federal funding? The same is true for our federal, state, and local law enforcement departments as it pertains to their missing-persons efforts. Someone will tell you that millions are spent every year on both these efforts (in law enforcement and private organizations). Yes, that's true. But, not enough is being spent. Not enough is being done.

What did we do after the 9-11 terrorist attacks? We went after the terrorists overseas and here at home. Our government created the new Department of Homeland Security, the Transportation Security Administration, and reorganized the government and military at the top levels to wage a war against terrorism. We hired thousands more federal officers, investigators, intelligence analysts, and covert operatives. We have spent trillions of dollars on the "war on terrorism" here at home, in Afghanistan and Iraq, and around the world to hunt down suspected terrorists and prevent future attacks. The same can be said for the "war on drugs".

Our government can do the same when it comes to a new and improved national missing-persons program. More innocent children and adults are brutally assaulted and murdered right here at home by these animals and monsters than are attacked by domestic or international terrorists. More lives and families are being destroyed by the animals and monsters than drugs.

Isn't that part of why our federal government established the Department of Homeland Security (DHS) in 2003? DHS is intended to protect our citizens here at home and abroad (overseas). This includes the Federal Bureau of Investigation (FBI). Both agencies exist to protect our country, government, and its citizens. Let's turn our attention and focus on stopping this *deadly epidemic* in America. I know we can do it!

By the way, the investigative arm of DHS changed names from Office of Investigations to "Homeland Security Investigation," or the three-letter acronym "HSI." HSI still falls under the Immigration and Customs Enforcement (ICE). Investigative responsibilities related to HSI include Human Smuggling, Human Trafficking, Operation Predator/Child Exploitation, and Cyber Crime. Other investigative and jurisdictional authority includes International Gangs, Identity and Benefit Fraud, Narcotics Trafficking, Money Laundering, and much, much more.

Along with the FBI, HSI is the largest federal investigative agency in the government with incredible resources and talent. Together they have thousands of Special Agents (criminal investigators) and Intelligence Analysts working counterterrorism and narcotics. Only a handful of agents and analysts are assigned to work missing-persons at a national level. This will be important later. Know that state and local governments receive millions of dollars and substantial resources every year from the federal government, DHS, and FBI for our national security here at home. But, not enough for missing persons. Not near enough.

What will all the skeptics say right this moment? *"There isn't any more money available."* *"We already have programs in place."* Yes, there is plenty of money, and no, we don't have a good enough program in place. What we lack is true leadership and vision from our legislators and government officials for a new and innovative national missing-persons program. Let's push for that together, as parents.

The first step for our leaders is to recognize that this problem is a deadly epidemic and then to make it a top priority for our nation. The next step is combating these sadistic abusers and killers in the same manner we now combat "terrorism"—with vigor and innovation. This will not only include an innovated national missing-persons program, but it will include *new* laws that will permanently remove the monsters from society once and for all.

I'm not getting off track, just changing tracks. Some people will argue that our jails and prisons are overcrowded as it is. This is very true, and every federal and state legislator (politician) knows that this is because of our antiquated and unfair drug sentencing laws, including the ridiculous "three strikes" sentencing law for *minor* drug offenses.

Why does a drug user or trafficker need to be locked up for twenty or thirty years when each offense involved *ounces* of marijuana? Not pounds or tons, but ounces. Why does a person caught with a few grams of "crack" cocaine go to prison much longer than someone caught with the same amount of cocaine? Or heroin and similar drugs for that matter? Are crack, cocaine, and heroin addictive? Yes. So is alcohol.

Do we really need to keep people in prison for twenty or thirty years for possessing ounces of marijuana and grams of illegal narcotics? This topic has been discussed at the highest levels of government for decades and has been ignored. We can stop overcrowding in our prisons with good common sense and a stroke of the pen. The problem is that our politicians simply do not have the will or courage to deal with the potential political backlash.

Get caught with just a little too much of these drugs three times and a person may be in jail longer than the alcoholic who murders an innocent family while drinking and driving. Oh, wait. That's not murder—it's negligent manslaughter. Or whatever legal defense can be whipped up and pulled out of a hat. It is cheaper for our courts and prisons to treat both the addiction and the cause than it is to simply lock up millions of *petty* drug abusers and so-called traffickers for twenty to thirty years. Remember, I said that these are the people using and trafficking in grams and ounces, not pounds and kilograms.

Back on the main track. We need to attack these "other terrorists" here at home with the same advanced strategies, technology, and techniques we have developed and now use overseas to combat terrorism. We need to protect our children and families the same way we protect our embassy personnel and service members overseas. Again, the same is true for our war on drugs. We spend billions every year on overseas personnel and resources to combat drug trafficking and smuggling.

I have seen both sides of the **War on Terrorism** and the **War on Drugs** overseas and at home. They in fact have worked at varying degrees and levels. We now need a **War on Predators**. We just need to shift the *focus* of the White House and Congress. We need to do the same with our state legislators and our governors and mayors. The focus needs to be on protecting American families here at home. Remember that term, War on Predators.

It is safe to say that these violent criminals and sexual predators have collectively killed as many innocent Americans in this country as foreign and domestic terrorists. A lot more. It is troublesome how our government and news media sensationalize terrorism at home while not placing enough emphasis on our missing children and adults. Try being abducted and brutalized and see how terrorizing that can be.

People have no real idea of the pain and suffering these victims endure while in captivity—not to mention the inconceivable heartache suffered by parents, spouses, and families. Try to imagine for just a moment a young child or teenager being kidnapped and then brutally and sexually abused. Our government places a lot of emphasis on Prisoners of War and Missing in Action. What about the POWs and MIAs right here at home?

After you learn more about this monumental national problem, contact your federal representatives in the US Congress and the President of the United States. Contact your state legislators in your General Assembly. Contact your governor, mayor, and local commissioners or council members. Demand they do more about this national *epidemic*. Tell them to start a *War on Predators* here at home. Tell them you want them to support and fund these missing-persons programs instead of pet projects and foreign governments.

The government needs to better fund NCMEC (children), ICMEC (international), LBTH (adults), and NCEA (elderly). They need to better fund and coordinate the Amber Alert, Silver Alert, and Code Adam programs. I'll talk more about these organizations and programs later. Most importantly, they need to fund and bring together all the different state agencies and missing-persons programs into one effective national program.

Do your local, state, and federal representatives even know and understand the magnitude of this epidemic? Do they know the numbers and statistics in their home state or local district? Do they know law enforcement departments are not capable of handling every call with the same scrutiny? Maybe not, but are you willing to tell them? Send them a copy of this book along with a personal letter.

Let's look at some government spending by both the US Congress and state general assemblies. These are programs and projects from which tax-payer dollars can be diverted to an advanced national missing-persons program.

Every year our President and Congress spend billions of our taxpayer dollars on *foreign aid* and assistance (both economic and military), but neglect our serious problems here at home. When I say "neglect," I mean that they are doing something, but not enough.

How much of our money does our federal government spend on foreign aid and assistance? On average **$60 billion a year**. Well, there is one source of money for Congress to allocate to a new and better national missing-persons program.

Every year our president and Congress spend billions of our taxpayer dollars on *pork barrel* and *wasteful earmarks*. Keep in mind not all earmarks are wasteful. How much do they spend every year on pork barrel and wasteful earmarks? An estimated **$20 billion a year**. In 2010, approximately 9,129 state projects cost federal taxpayers $16.5 billion. In 2009, this figure was over $19 billion. A government watchdog organization reported pork-barrel waste to be as high as $23 billion a year.

This particular kind of wasteful spending is sometimes referred to as "pet projects" that help politicians receive higher campaign donations for reelection. It is nothing new, and has been addressed by our own members of Congress and the White House for decades.

Together, foreign aid and pork barrel totals about $80 billion a year. All this wasteful spending during a five year financial crisis. Again, no need to argue exact figures. It is HUGE! It is madness! It is irresponsible! Why don't we propose that the government dedicate just some of that money to save innocent lives? Even half that amount would be helpful. How about $40 billion? We haven't even discussed our defense budget, just foreign aid and pork barrel. Our entire Department of Defense budget is usually around $1 trillion a year. How about a few billion from there?

What about wasteful pork barrel and earmarks at the *state* level? I don't think anyone knows. State legislators typically refuse to reveal these figures—despite official Freedom of Information requests by investigative journalists

CHAPTER 2: GENERAL INFORMATION

and private organizations. There are not enough watchdog organizations to track all fifty states. The amount spent by our state legislators and governors every year can be in the billions for each state, or that amount can be over a trillion dollars when combining all states. Listen! I know I'm leaving out our US territories and commonwealths, but this is just general information.

A few years ago we heard news reports that the federal government spent almost $880 billion on bailouts and stimulus to help corporate America, which included financial institutions (Wall Street) and automakers. How many people know the true figure is now estimated to be between $14 and $16 trillion?

We allegedly gave trillions to both US and *foreign* financial institutions during these bailouts. Investigative journalists and several members of Congress have demanded a full audit of the Federal Reserve System (Fed) to determine who received the money and how much.

Did Corporate America and the foreign banks learn anything from this world-wide financial crisis? No! Many corporate executive officers (CEOs) thumbed their noses at the government, and it was business as usual after the handouts. Did the government turn around and suggest giving them more bailouts? Yes, they did. Wow!

By the way the Fed has refused to complete a full audit and disclose this information by simply claiming the information is too sensitive. Many members of Congress and most Americans support a full audit. However, the President and Congress as a whole have refused to vote together and force the Fed to complete an audit. Why? What is going on in our government?

Why mention any of this? To show that the government does have the money and the means to create a new and effective missing-persons program at the national level. Let's suggest to the president and Congress that they divert half the amount of foreign aid and pork barrel every year to a new and improved national missing-persons program.

That $40 billion can now be used to save American citizens from serious harm and death at the hands of hardened criminals and sexual predators. That's an extra $780 million per state every year versus the few million they now receive. At the same time, let's demand our state legislators divert more money to state programs for missing children and adults. Will that extra $40 billion be needed every year? No! Once the program is up and running, it will take a lot less funding to sustain.

Bottom line: The government is not adequately investing in a national missing-persons program that will save *thousands* of lives and trauma every year.

In 2009, the federal government unexpectedly and without explanation stopped funding the National Center for Missing Adults (NCMA). NCMA was later absorbed by Let's Bring Them Home (LBTH). Both NCMEC and LBTH receive some federal funding, but not enough. They are heavily dependent on private donations. Why should either of these organizations rely on private funding or volunteers? This is insane. The government should be fully funding all four of these national support organizations,

Then there are the **Amber Alert** and **Silver Alert** programs. What about **Code Adam**? How about the **National Missing and Unidentified Persons System (NamUs)** and the **National Crime Information Center's (NCIC) Missing-Person File**? These programs are also in dire need of more funding and resources. Research and learn more about these programs as well.

What about starting a national television program, like America's Most Wanted? The government can call it, "*America's Missing Children and Adults.*" I'll talk more about this later.

Is this national epidemic not just as important as our quest for a broader and more costly national health-care program? In fact, couldn't a better missing-persons program be considered *preventive medicine*, as it relates to physical and mental health? Is protecting a young child, teenager, or adult from serious injury not as important as having access to a personal physician to treat injuries and diseases?

When I make this statement, keep in mind that all hospitals must provide the same emergency medical care to a patient with or without medical insurance. So, everyone in the United States has access to emergency medical treatment and care. Isn't a person who suddenly turns up missing an emergency?

When you contact your federal and state representatives (will you?) they may tell you, *"There is only so much money to go around."* First, remind them the President and Congress have a constitutional mandate to protect our citizens at home and abroad. Second, remind them this is a deadly national epidemic, which involves interstate and international crimes. Inform them that criminal and sexual predators kill far more people here at home than domestic terrorists. Last, remind them of the $80 billion being spent every year on foreign aid and pork-barrel.

Chapter 3

HIRING A PRIVATE INVESTIGATOR

What is a private investigator? Forget about those characters we have all seen on television and in movies. The government has detectives and agents who investigate crimes that are a violation of federal, state, and local laws. Defense attorneys and private investigators will help if you have been wrongly accused of a criminal or civil violation. Attorneys and PIs can also help you with other personal matters, i.e., missing-persons, harassment, theft and fraud, etc.

Think of it like this: If you are arrested and charged with a crime you did not commit, who is going to investigate that matter on your behalf? Your attorney and a private investigator. A good attorney will not only use a PI, but will rely on that investigator's expertise. An attorney is not a trained investigator.

Private investigators work for the private sector and do essentially the same thing as detectives. Many PIs work for criminal and civil attorneys and some work for insurance companies. But, most important, they work for *YOU*. The vast majority of PIs are true professionals. But like any profession, there are some bad apples. I'll tell you how to find a good one.

It may sound a little corny, but private investigators can be considered the "seekers of information and the truth," and most of them are very good at what they do.

There is nothing wrong with hiring a legitimate and qualified private investigator to help you find your missing loved one. The sooner you hire a PI the better. Why hire a PI to help you protect or locate your loved one? I'll explain this, as well as some obstacles you may encounter.

Some law enforcement officers and detectives will disagree about hiring and working with a private investigator. If they do object to your hiring one, ask them why and listen closely to their argument or opinion. Opinions are just that: someone else's views that are often biased and/or wrong.

If you encounter this situation, ask yourself if the police officer or detective is making a legitimate argument. Ask them detailed questions, and then you decide. This is a serious matter, and it is about you finding your loved one immediately; it is not about jurisdictional disputes or egos.

A lot of private investigators are former law enforcement officers or detectives with vast training and experience. Many PIs may not have prior law enforcement experience, but they have extensive experience in conducting missing-person investigations, if not experience with simply finding people who are hiding.

A private investigator does not have the same restrictions and constraints as most detectives and police departments. They do not have to deal with a chain of command and other bureaucratic obstacles that delay an investigation. PIs are not bound by set hours and overtime. A PI may need to seek international approval from certain government officials in some instances, but in most cases foreign travel is not an issue. It is certainly not a bureaucratic or budget issue. Let a detective tell his boss he needs to travel to the Bahamas or Peru to interview some witnesses or check out a few suspects or locations and see what happens. I know—I have been on both sides of the fence on all these issues.

A private investigator is able to quickly travel anywhere around the state and country at will, and can easily travel internationally. He does not need several layers of approval or budget restraints to contend with. In most instances the PI will not have a heavy caseload and can easily dedicate more time and effort to finding your missing loved one. He is not directed to investigate cases with a lesser priority. He is not on the clock. I have seen all of this this as well.

A good detective and private investigator can make a very effective team. Most law enforcement officers and detectives in fact know that PIs have helped police departments and victims/clients solve many complicated cases, yet the barriers and biases still exist. The key is getting the detective and PI to work together. This means overcoming internal police policies or prejudices.

There may be an internal "policy" prohibiting detectives from working with private investigators, but it's not likely. If so, that police chief or sheriff should be fired for ineptitude. It may be permitted and the detective may not have a problem working with a PI, but his supervisor might have a problem (prejudice). That supervisor is being incompetent.

The law enforcement officer or detective may be restricted in terms of what information they can share with a private investigator. That's acceptable, if that is in fact true. If the information does not violate a right to privacy or financial privacy act (law) it can be shared. Even if it does, government attorneys (counsel) can obtain waivers. Even if information is classified as national security it can be shared. I know. I have a national security clearance. These issues need to be ironed out. You may very well become the intermediary.

Would I hire a PI if my loved one disappeared? Absolutely! That PI can work with the police or work alone. The PI will definitely be working with and for me. I would want to find my child or wife as *fast* as possible. We know the reason why, correct?

What I just said may cause a few hurt feelings, but those of us in law enforcement know this problem exists. I have witnessed interagency and departmental rivalries that have caused major cases to disintegrate. It even exists internally. I have seen offices and squads from the same department or agency fail to work together. It is both petty and a pity because the bad guy gets away and the innocent suffers.

Here are a few important tips to know about hiring a private investigator. Some states require that a PI be licensed and some do not. Some states require that a PI be bonded and insured and some do not. Some PIs may operate out of an office building and some may work out of their home. None of this really matters, unless they are violating state regulation. When you speak to a PI, ask them about state regulations, and simply make sure they are in compliance. If they are not, that is a bad indicator. Make sure you verify everything the PI tells you. I already told you, I do not accept everything as gospel, even from the authorities or the so-called experts.

To find out about a certain private investigator, contact your Secretary of State's office and ask which department oversees private investigators. There is usually a regulatory board that oversees certain professions, e.g., private protection services, medical, attorneys, accountants, etc.

Your Secretary of State may have a professional board that oversees all security professionals to include private investigators, alarm companies, armed and unarmed security guards, executive protection (body guards), counterintelligence services, etc. Yes, you can even hire counterintelligence services to sweep your home, office, and telephones for electronic listening devices or "bugs." Do you know how easy it is to bug your phone, office or home?

Don't always rely on Internet searches to find the state agency that oversees these professions. One state in particular regulates private investigators under their Department of Agriculture. That's odd. Other states may have a Private Protection Services Board (PPSB) and some may not. An online search may be difficult. Make a phone call and ask the Secretary of State if the PI or business you are interested in meets all requirements and if they are in good standing. Ask if there are any complaints on file and the outcomes.

If you decide to hire a particular private investigator, ask to meet with them in person. The initial phone call is like a resume, nothing more than a screening. It's that interview that is important. Most PIs will not charge for the initial consultation, which may be from thirty minutes to an hour. Ask them about this initial consultation. Then ask them about their billing. How much do they charge by the hour and for expenses? Do they require a retainer, and if so how much? You can always discuss these details at the initial meeting, but they should be willing to answer basic questions over the telephone. If not, ask yourself why.

When you meet the private investigator, the first thing you will ask about is their personal qualifications for helping you locate your missing child or loved one. Find out about their professional education, training, and experience in this area.

I always suggest people write down their questions before any meeting and then take notes during the meeting. Don't ask the questions over the telephone. It is better to hear their responses in person and evaluate the potential costs and a future relationship.

Here are some tips on asking people questions in general. Wow! All this free advice. I always find that short, open-ended questions work best; then, let a person talk. Look at them and listen carefully to what they say and how they say it. Watch their face for any distinguishable expressions. Most people have a tendency to do all the talking when interviewing. That is not how you learn things.

Two examples of questions you might want to ask a PI are, "What qualifies you to conduct a missing-person investigation?" and "What do you think about the local police department and their investigators when it comes to missing-person investigations?" These are two critical questions that require discussion and need personal evaluation. Why are you asking that second question? I'll explain.

When you talk to a private investigator, ask them not only about their training and experience, but also ask them questions about their working relationship with a particular police department and the missing-person squad. Do they have a good relationship with the local authorities or a bad relationship? Does the PI sound professional or hostile? You want a PI who is passionate about his work, but not unprofessional.

When you talk to someone pay close attention to *what* they say and *how* they say it. First, it is the polite thing to do. Second, you can tell a lot about a person and what they are saying by watching their eyes and facial expressions. The same applies to their voice. Sometimes the inflection of sarcasm in their voice may not be that obvious, but it may be readable in their face.

The next thing you should discuss is the details of their billing. How much do they charge by the hour and for expenses? Do they require a retainer? How much time will they be able to devote to your case? If a PI has a heavy caseload or other commitments, this could be a problem. I would want to hire someone who would work for me full time beginning *immediately*. I would want to hire someone with professional training and experience. I would want to hire someone who gives me a good first impression and who is confident. Hey! Don't be afraid to ask for references; and more important, follow up on them.

A good private investigator is in the information business, but many PIs are also good at finding people, solving crimes, and coming up with solutions. A good PI will offer personal advice from an outside perspective. I once heard a PI say he did not give personal advice. Why not? It is up to you to decide if you accept anyone's advice. Never ignore free advice or suggestions; just sort through it and determine what is true and relevant for you. Then verify the information to determine if it is accurate and factual through basic research. Always ask a lot of questions to obtain all the details. Always double check your facts and verify information.

CHAPTER 3: HIRING A PRIVATE INVESTIGATOR

Now, having said all this about private investigators, I called one missing-persons "organization" to ask questions, and the man on the other end was very hesitant and vague at first. I told him I was a PI and what I was doing. He opened up a little bit more and told me he was a PI and worked with a few others on locating missing persons. I hung up the telephone and threw his information in the trash. Why did he try to represent himself online as an organization? Why was he so hesitant to talk to me and answer my questions at first? There may be a legitimate answer, but I went with my gut feeling and dismissed him. I prefer people who are open and honest.

Remember what I said about your gut feelings…your instincts? If someone sounds suspicious, they probably are. There are so many scam artists in this world that you have to be careful and you have to ask a lot of questions. When someone tells you something, you need to independently verify what you have been told. This is easy to do if you ask enough questions, and, more important, the right questions.

A good private investigator can also help you with your personal and family security plan. As I said, PIs are in the business of information collection and personal security. When you want someone or something checked out, hire a reputable PI. Let them do the work and take any risks for you. Don't play detective yourself. You can make mistakes and create a lot of problems. You may even get yourself hurt snooping around.

Do you feel you need to find out something about a fiancé or fiancée, or even a new boyfriend or girlfriend? What about that person you met online or through a dating service? Private investigators can check a variety of government and business records, to include marriage and divorce. I would want to know if that new person in my life has a criminal record or serious financial problems. They may have prior criminal records for violence or fraud; or civil records on file for bankruptcy and monetary judgments.

Crucial advice: Hire a private investigator to check out anyone new in your life. Better to be safe than sorry.

Private investigators can conduct pre-employment and employment background investigations as well. What about a contractor or new employee you hire to work around your home? What about a strange neighbor? If you feel there is the need to know something about a particular person, for whatever reason, then hire a good PI to investigate. Why not? Don't just let any stranger into your home or into your life. What about that strange neighbor who keeps inviting your children over to his house?

In my lifetime I have seen some really smart people make some really bad choices when it comes to major decisions; for example, investments. Hire someone you can trust to help you and someone who can be objective and give you good advice. Hire someone who knows how to dig up information and facts. That will not always be true of a partner or close friend. Don't believe everything you are told, especially when it comes to money. There are two category of people who want your money—the IRS and everyone else.

Bottom line: If a loved one turns up missing, consider hiring a private investigator for all the reasons discussed. Don't wait too long! Sit down and personally talk to at least three PIs you feel may be qualified to assist you. Invite them to your home. Find out their qualifications and check up on them. Determine exactly how much they will charge you and how these charges and expenses will be documented and controlled. Don't be shy about this. Ask them about their *"investigative plan."* What will they do first, and how will they proceed from there? Give them a copy of your loved one's Biographical Form to get started. This all needs to be accomplished immediately. Perhaps you may want to meet some PIs today for future contact. Be prepared!

Crucial advice: Contact two or more private investigators now and check them out thoroughly. Make sure they have the qualifications and experience to conduct missing-person investigations. I would suggest one local PI and one from a larger firm.

Chapter 4

STATISTICS AND NUMBERS TO THINK ABOUT

Let's take a look at some statistics and numbers as they relate to violent and sexual offenders. These figures came from various sources and reports found on the Internet. Again, the actual numbers are not important; it is the sheer magnitude of the problem that is central for us to realize and for the government to tackle. The purpose of this chapter is to give you some facts so that you will understand the seriousness of this topic.

Violent Criminals on the Loose

In the year 2009, according to the Federal Bureau of Investigation's (FBI) Uniformed Crime Reporting (UCR) program, there were an estimated **1.3 million "violent crimes"** committed nationwide. These crimes included four categories in which "violence" was used:

15,241 murders

88,097 forcible rapes

806,843 aggravated assaults (usually meaning serious harm and involving weapons)

408,217 robberies (usually meaning serious harm and involving weapons)

In 2009, the Bureau of Justice Statistics (BJS) reported an estimated **4.3 million "violent crimes."** This is a separate and different report from the FBI's UCR. Along with aggravated assaults, the BJS included a fifth category: "simple assaults" with violence.

Keep in mind, a lot of violent crimes will go unreported. The true figures are probably much higher than 1.3 billion and 4.3 billion.

So, let's just go with the higher statistic on violence and state that on average of 4.3 million violent crimes are being committed every year in America. We can safely assume this is not one person committing all these violent acts. So, let's just say there are about four million violent offenders out there in our society.

Four million comes to an average of eighty-six thousand violent offenders per state. There are over three thousand counties across America, so that averages out to over **thirteen hundred violent offenders per county**. What are the odds you will cross paths with one of these hardened criminals any given day of the week?

What are the chances you or one of your loved ones will encounter a violent offender? The chances are very high. I read one report that stated over **56 percent of violent offenders are repeat offenders** (*Recidivist* is the technical term.) Apparently, over half the violent offenders did not learn the first time, and neither have the prosecutors and judges who keep letting them go.

Another FBI report stated that serial killings are a rare occurrence and are estimated to comprise less than 1 percent of all murders committed in any given year. So, think about this. **In 2009, if there were 15,241**

murders, then 1 percent makes a possible 152 serial killings in any given year or three serial killings per state.

The FBI also reported there have been approximately four hundred serial killers in the United States in the past century. The number of victims was estimated to be between 2,526 and to 3,850. Okay, that averages out to eight serial killers per state and fifty to seventy-seven victims per state.

Whatever the true figures are, serial killers and violent offenders represent a very real threat to us and our families. There will be some examples later.

According to a Department of Justice (DOJ) report, each year an estimated **one million women and 371,000 men are** *stalked* in the United States. These stalkers can include serial killers, individual offenders, sexual predators, home invaders, and gang members. Many acts of stalking and sexual violence occur on our university and college campuses. So, what are the odds of you or one of your loved ones is being stalked?

Crucial advice: When you are walking about, you want to display signs of active precaution that will cause the stalker to turn his attention elsewhere. This means you need to keep your eyes and head turning. Do in fact look at everything and everyone around you. Walk with confidence and purpose.

In the military and law enforcement, the terms *soft targets* and *hard targets* are frequently used to describe victims and vulnerable targets. You need to learn how to become a hard target, and the same goes for your loved ones. You also want your home and workplace to be hard targets.

Most criminals and predators will turn away from a hard target and pursue a soft target. If you learn how, you can decrease your odds of being attacked by displaying yourself and your family as threats to the stalker. That's a good role reversal.

What do you do when a loved one is living and going to school in another state and suddenly disappears? Hopefully you are prepared to take action.

Another Department of Justice (DOJ) study states that during a four-year period, **one in four college women will be victims of rape or attempted rape**. One in four!

The word *university* will apply to colleges, universities, prep-schools, technical institutes, and any other school of higher education. Here is a dose of hard reality. Most universities are not doing much about the problems on and around our campuses. They put on a good show and do a lot of talking, but what have they really done to protect our children?

The first step they should take is to get serious about alcohol and drugs. They should also look at how both relate to fraternity and sorority activities. I'm emphasizing the *illegal* use of alcohol and drugs on and around campus. I'm emphasizing the *abuse* of alcohol and drugs. The second step they need to take is to institute crime prevention and safety for their students on and off campus.

Argue all you want, but we all know, in general, that excessive drinking and use of drugs are major factors in violent and sexual offenses. As parents we may not be able to order our children to stop drinking and using drugs, but we can talk to them about moderation and safety. Teach them this saying: **"Everything in moderation."** This includes the obvious vices such as alcohol, drugs, and sex. But it can include almost any other aspect of our lives to include partying, shopping, watching TV, playing video games, Internet surfing, sleeping, eating M&Ms, etc. Everything in moderation. Maybe that applies to us adults as well.

As parents we can talk to our children about their sexual activities and dating. We can talk to them about taking security precautions where they live and where they travel. We can talk to them about date rape and date rape drugs. Don't be nervous or shy. Just study and rehearse your speech. Try not to yell and scream. Let the kids talk too.

We have all heard that argument about women dressing and acting provocatively. No woman deserves to be raped. Ever! However, use good

CHAPTER 4: STATISTICS AND NUMBERS TO THINK ABOUT

judgment based on the circumstances and your surroundings. Don't attract the attention of a sexual deviant. In addition to moderation, people need to use good common sense when it comes to crime and sexual prevention.

You wouldn't walk up to a supposedly tame bear and start poking him in the chest, would you? You might just push his "On" button. Would you go to bed at night and leave all your doors and windows wide open? I'm sure maniacs like Ted Bundy would appreciate the invitation.

Here is a nasty trick. Many universities and colleges will ignore crimes against students if they take place off the physical boundaries of the school grounds—even if multiple crimes are occurring in a string of fraternity and sorority houses or apartments a few feet from the boundary line. Universities may not report crimes against nonstudents. This deception lowers their annual crime statistics and numbers. I bet one of those morons would say it makes them look "better." Again, how many violent and sexual crimes go unreported and are not included in the annual crime reports?

Crucial advice: An Individual Protection Packet prepared for your university or college student living away from home is *extremely* important and must be kept updated. Their information will probably change every year.

More crucial advice: Students living away from home need to check in with a family member, loved one, or close friend as often as possible. More on that later.

This means you, as the parent, must take tough steps. Sit down with your children and talk to them about completing their protection packets. Keep them updated. Implement some of the rules we will talk about, with the first rule being: call someone and let them know who you are with, where you are, and what you are doing. It beats being raped, vanishing, or dying.

Let's read about a few cases involving serial killers just to understand who some of the monsters are and what they are capable of doing to innocent men, women, teenagers, and children. Keep in mind that even though the number of serial killers is estimated to be around 400 and the number of their victims is estimated to be between 2,526 and 3,850, in reality both figures are probably much higher. The number of serial killers roaming our country right now could be double that figure. The number of victims could be twice as much.

Rodney James Alcala, aka The Dating Game Killer — Alcala is a convicted rapist and serial killer. In 2010, he was sentenced to death in California. He was charged with five murders in that state and was to be indicted for two other murders in New York. The actual number of victims who were tortured and murdered is probably much higher, and many other possible victims were identified. At least ten. However, there was not enough evidence to include those victims in the charges. Keep in mind, he was known for torturing his victims before killing them.

Alcala appeared on the former television show, The Dating Game. Even though he won a date with one of the bachelorettes, she refused to go out with him, describing him as creepy. Alcala also served in the US Army and was discharged after being diagnosed with a number of antisocial personality disorders. Alcala was a graduate of a well-known university and supposedly had a genius IQ level. He held various jobs that allowed him to have access to young girls and women, to include becoming a professional fashion photographer.

As early as 1968, he was investigated for luring an eight-year-old girl into his apartment, where he beat and raped her. After fleeing the state of California, he went to New York where he enrolled in school and held a job in Connecticut as a counselor for young children under different aliases. He was eventually found guilty and convicted of raping and beating the young girl in California, but was released from prison after being declared "rehabilitated."

CHAPTER 4: STATISTICS AND NUMBERS TO THINK ABOUT

In other brutal cases, Alcala was convicted and sentenced, but his convictions were overturned on legal technicalities. After being convicted and sentenced once again to prison for yet another sex crime, he was again determined rehabilitated and released. In most cases where Alcala was arrested or sent to prison, he almost immediately committed more violent sex crimes, including murder, upon his release. If he could have only been stopped earlier.

Herbert Richard Baumeister — In 1996, at least eleven bodies were found buried on Baumeister's property in Indiana. He is suspected of killing twenty young males, most of them believed to be gay. Baumeister had a history of bizarre behavior dating back to his youth. Throughout his life he was diagnosed with having personality disorders. Baumeister was married and had three children. He was a successful businessman and considered a wealthy and affluent member of his community. Many considered him to be well liked. However, his wife was terrified of his unpredictable behavior.

In addition to the eleven bodies found on his property, Baumeister was suspected of killing at least nine other men. After the bodies were found on his property, he escaped to Ontario, Canada. In 1996, Baumeister committed suicide before he could be captured and face trial.

Twenty sadistic murders. How many actual murders did he commit? How many murders did he attempt? Of the bodies found on his ranch, only five could be identified. How many people were murdered and still classified as missing?

Theodore Robert "Ted" Bundy — Bundy is one of America's most notorious serial killers. It is suspected he kidnapped, raped, tortured, and murdered between thirty to thirty-five young women during the mid-1970s to the early-1980s throughout six different states. The actual number could be as high as one hundred. His first murder may have occurred when he was a teenager. His monstrous crimes also included acts of necrophilia, sexually abusing dead bodies. Some of his victims he decapitated and many he sodomized. Bundy was considered to be an intelligent, handsome, and charismatic person.

Bundy graduated from the University of Washington (UW) as an honor student and attended the University of Utah Law School. He majored in psychology and law and studied Chinese. Bundy attended other universities, and later visited universities to find his victims. While at UW, young women began disappearing at the rate of one per month. He had several serious relationships with well-respected women, and it was thought he had the opportunity for outstanding careers in the legal profession and politics. Bundy appeared to be your ordinary well-rounded good guy. He could be that guy standing next to you with a nice smile. One of the *others*.

Many of the young women he raped, tortured, and savagely murdered were kidnapped from public locations, and with some he broke into their homes. Others were hitchhikers. Some of his sexual assaults and murders included teenagers as young as twelve years of age and college students. Many of these young girls survived for weeks before succumbing to their brutal injuries. Some were left to die in their homes and some he abandoned in remote locations to die alone. This is why I emphasize being able to find your loved one in hours as opposed to days or weeks later. It can be done.

After his arrest and during various pre-trial motions, much evidence presented against Bundy was ruled inadmissible and thrown out of court. Twice during his incarceration Bundy escaped and committed more murders. Did he escape to be free? No, he escaped so he could continue torturing, raping, and murdering innocent girls and women. After fleeing Chicago, Bundy made his way to the Florida State University. He broke into an FSU sorority house and attacked four women in that one evening. All of them were savagely attacked and two murdered. There were around thirty other occupants in the building, yet no one heard anything. How is that possible?

Bundy was ultimately convicted of the murders, burglaries, and assaults that took place at FSU. Bundy was interviewed by several law enforcement

CHAPTER 4: STATISTICS AND NUMBERS TO THINK ABOUT

agents and doctors. He stated that at first he was just an amateur killer who reacted impulsively to eliminate his victims. Bundy said he later became a professional predator and killer. He killed because he liked it. Bundy was executed in 1989.

Charles Ng and Leonard Lake — Ng and Lake were suspected of murdering between twelve and twenty-five people, to include women, men, teenagers, and two infants over a period of two years. Many of their victims were married and had families and had been kidnapped or lured to their cabin home. Leonard Lake's own brother and a few friends became victims as well.

Charles Ng, who came from a wealthy family, met Leonard Lake and his second wife after they were arrested for theft. After serving a prison sentence, they reunited and together filmed many of their incredibly violent assaults in a hideaway cabin. It was in this cabin where they brutally and sadistically raped, terrorized, and tortured their victims. Some of the women were forced to become sex slaves, hoping to save the lives of their babies and loved ones. Buried on the property were numerous bodies to include two families, including their babies.

Lake eventually committed suicide after being captured by police. Ng was ultimately convicted and sentenced to death in California in 1999. Ng's lengthy trial and his appeal against the death sentence took almost fourteen years and cost the state of California around $14 million. Keep in mind the evidence included the bodies being found on their property, gruesome video tapes, photographs, and a personal journal of their accounts. This is a mockery of our judicial system perpetrated by out-of-control defense attorneys, prosecutors, magistrates, and judges. Fourteen years and over $14 million to prosecute this one animal.

Henry Lee Lucas and **Ottis Toole** — Lucas, a drifter, was convicted of murdering 189 people. Lucas led police to the bodies of 246 victims, but he was convicted of murdering only 189 people. Lucas later confessed to killing around six hundred people over a period of three decades, but police believed only 350 of his confessions to be credible. His murders included women and men, both teenagers and adults.

Lucas's first victim is believed to be his prostitute mother, whom he stabbed and killed in a drunken brawl. Lucas was convicted of second-degree murder and served only ten years in prison for that crime. Lucas died in prison in 2001.

Because of our judicial system, Lucas was released from prison, possibly based on overcrowding, and allowed to continue his killing spree around the country. Anywhere from 190 to six hundred victims could have been spared had he been sent away to prison for life or executed.

Ottis Toole is a serial killer, kidnapper, rapist, and arsonist who supposedly cannibalized some of his victims. Toole was married for a short time and divorced when his wife learned he was a homosexual. Toole and Lucas met and became lovers. Tool confessed he participated in at least 108 murders with Lucas. Toole was believed to be the murderer of six-year-old Adam Walsh in Florida. Adam's father is John Walsh, the former host of America's Most Wanted. Toole died in prison in 1996.

John Wayne Gacy, Jr. — Gacy sexually assaulted and murdered at least thirty-three teenage boys and young men between the years 1972 and 1978. Gacy often performed as a clown at parties and events. He was married and had two children before divorcing and remarrying a second time. Gacy was charged with various sexual crimes over the years and, again, justice failed to keep him in prison.

There are hundreds of other cases involving serial killers and many more that are not classified as serial killers simply because the evidence did not exist to match the definition. A serial killer is usually someone who has killed over three people over a period of one month or more. Another definition states a serial killer must be involved in two or more murders that were separate events and committed by one person.

CHAPTER 4: STATISTICS AND NUMBERS TO THINK ABOUT

Serial killers are not the same as spree killers, who commit murders in two or more locations with no break in between. Wow! Isn't it strange how closely we study and classify violent and sadistic criminals and different types of crimes, and yet our legal system and our courts keep letting these monsters go free?

I wonder just how many serial and spree killers were never classified as such simply because the evidence did not provide proof or because we simply do not know how many killings they completed. I mentioned our poor judicial system. You really need to research how a hardened and career criminal can commit multiple monstrous crimes, yet his crimes cannot be revealed in separate trials because it may bias the juries. Incredible!

Bottom line: When a cold-blooded murderer is convicted of one intentional murder, he should be sentenced to life in prison or executed. This is not a debate about the death penalty. Our courts should never release these monsters back into society. If a criminal knowingly and intentionally takes an innocent life in cold blood they should be removed from society forever. It is as simple as that.

In some trials, prior offenses are accidently revealed and result in a mistrial (an error in judicial procedures), or a conviction and sentence being overturned. Let's just say a "brutal" kidnapper and rapist has been charged and convicted with two violent acts over a twenty-year period. One involved the kidnapping and brutal rape of a young female adult and one involved the kidnapping and brutal rape of a teenaged girl. Let's say the evidence is irrefutable, but somehow this monster serves time in both cases and each time he is released from prison, for whatever reason. This is insane!

Continuing with the above example, after our good prosecutors and judges have freed this monster to once again prey on innocent people and families, this sadistic kidnapper and rapist is caught committing his third sadistic act. But this time the child dies. The courts will possibly not allow the jurors to know about the two prior acts because this might prejudice their discussions and final verdict. It's even possible their past crimes may not be considered for sentencing this rapist and murderer yet a third time. Believe it or not, similar cases have occurred.

Missing Children

Here are some more statistics from the US Department of Justice (DOJ) and the National Center for Missing and Exploited Children (NCMEC) on missing children and kidnappings:

797,500 children (age seventeen and younger) were reported missing in a one-year period of time studied, resulting in an average of 2,185 children being reported missing each day.

203,900 children were the victims of *family abductions.*

58,200 children were the victims of *nonfamily abductions.*

115 children were the victims of *"stereotypical" kidnapping.* Of the stereotypical kidnappings, it was reported that 40 percent of the children were murdered and another 4 percent were never recovered.

So, let's just look at the actual abductions, or kidnappings. If there were a total of **262,215 child kidnappings** (family, nonfamily, and stereotypical) in one year, then what happened to the other 535, 285 children reported missing?

Can we assume the other 535,285 who were reported as missing were runaways or involved in an accident? How many were in fact kidnapped but not classified as such? Perhaps they were manipulated into disappearing from home or their loved ones, so they were not categorized as such. I don't know.

How many of the 535,285 were physically harmed, emotionally or mentally traumatized, sexually abused, or never seen again? How many

CHAPTER 4: STATISTICS AND NUMBERS TO THINK ABOUT

were forced into child pornography and prostitution? How many were murdered? Any of these acts are horrendous.

According to reports, of the 58,315 children kidnapped by both "nonfamily" members and considered stereotypical, most were sexually assaulted and many of them were either murdered or never seen again. Do you know what? That averages out to be over 159 children a day. That is unacceptable.

Of the 203,900 family-member kidnappings, how many were physically or mentally harmed? How many have never been seen again? How many were murdered or accidently killed? Just because the victim was classified as being kidnapped by a relative doesn't mean they do not need to be found, and as quickly as possible. This is another reason to have a complete Individual Protection Packet on each of your children.

A few years ago, I saw a FBI report that stated that **150,000 missing children were classified as "abandoned"** and **250,000 missing children were classified as "runaways."** Again, keep in mind many others may not be reported to the authorities.

What happens to all these children who are abandoned and run away? How many of them are seriously harmed, sexually abused, or vanish, never to be seen again? How many are forced into child pornography and prostitution? How many are murdered or die?

As of December 31, 2008, the National Crime Information Center's (NCIC's) Missing-Person File reported there were **102,764 active missing-person records**. Juveniles under the age of eighteen accounted for 51,054 (49.7 percent) of the records and 12,648 (12.3 percent) were records for juveniles between the ages of eighteen and twenty. What about adults and the elderly? I couldn't find out this information.

Whatever the true answers and exact numbers of these staggering statistics, the bottom line is that **over 262,000 children were reportedly *kidnapped***

in one year. This averages more than seven hundred kidnappings a day or one child kidnapped every two minutes.

Our country should have a sophisticated and well-coordinated program that will allow us to find these children as quickly as possible. If our government will not recognize this responsibility, then we as parents and guardians must ensure we have the means to find and rescue our children as quickly as possible.

Another official report states an estimated **one hundred thousand children are the victims of** *commercial child prostitution* **and** *child trafficking.* Are we some third-world country?

Most of us are aware of Amber Alerts (named after nine-year-old Amber Hagerman) that are issued both statewide and nationwide for missing children. According to official reports, in the year 2009 Amber Alerts were entered into the system involving 263 missing children. There are specific criteria for entering an Amber alert. What are they? If your child turns up missing, will your child be excluded? You need to research this topic for an answer.

Keep in mind there are an estimated 262,000 child kidnappings a year. The above numbers don't add up. What happened to the others? Is there another national missing-person reporting system, or were the others in some sort of state database? Can states share their information in an efficient and timely manner? I don't know.

We learned there is a statistic indicating that the average time for the police to respond to a missing child report, collect all the information, and take action is two hours—two HOURS! According to an official report, only one third of Amber Alerts are entered into the system within one to three hours, but the other two thirds (of alerts) took between four and twelve hours to enter into the system. Any time over one hour is too long.

These systems and programs need more funding so information and details can be immediately entered and distributed countrywide. Law

CHAPTER 4: STATISTICS AND NUMBERS TO THINK ABOUT

enforcement and investigative agencies should be able to access and update this information at all levels instantly. Our federal government recently invested billions in a computer system allowing medical personnel to share records and information instantaneously. What about missing persons? Personally, I don't want my medical records found by just anyone. However, this is smart when it comes to missing persons, because we do want their records to be found by everyone.

Human Trafficking for Labor and Sexual Profit

Most people think of *human trafficking* as a foreign problem. Did you know that human trafficking, also known as *trafficking in persons*, is a serious problem right here in the United States, and growing by leaps and bounds? Many of these cases involve sex crimes, such as forced prostitution and pornography (adult and children), and the victims are American citizens—our children.

According to the Trafficking Victims Protection Act of 2000 (TVPA), human trafficking has occurred if a person was induced to perform labor or a commercial sex act through force, fraud, or coercion. Any person *under age eighteen* who performs a commercial sex act is considered a victim of human trafficking, regardless of whether force, fraud, or coercion was present. Under the age of eighteen years! What about those eighteen and nineteen years of age? Come on—those are our children. More on that age distinction later.

Federally funded task forces opened **2,515 suspected incidents of human trafficking** for investigation between January 2008 and June 2010. (Keep in mind these are incidents that are reported.)

Among the 389 incidents "confirmed" to be human trafficking:

>   There were 488 suspects and 527 victims.

> More than half of the confirmed *labor trafficking* victims were age twenty-five or older, compared to 13 percent of confirmed *sex trafficking* victims.
>
> Confirmed sex trafficking victims were more likely to be white (26 percent) or black (40 percent), compared to labor trafficking victims, who were more likely to be Hispanic (63 percent) or Asian (17 percent).
>
> Four-fifths of victims (83 percent) in confirmed sex trafficking incidents were identified as US citizens, while most confirmed labor trafficking victims were identified as undocumented aliens (67 percent) or qualified aliens (28 percent).
>
> Most confirmed human trafficking *suspects* were male (81 percent). More than half (62 percent) of confirmed sex trafficking suspects were identified as black, while confirmed labor trafficking suspects were more likely to be identified as Hispanic (48 percent).

Now, keep in mind that even though the above report claims there were 2,515 suspected incidents of human trafficking, another official report stated an estimated one hundred thousand children are the victims of commercial child prostitution and child trafficking.

Bottom line: In addition to crimes by violent offenders, we can see that **a large number of victims are abducted or held against their will by criminals for commercial profit**. This involves child and adult labor, but even far worse, child and adult pornography and prostitution.

Yes, there are evil people in this world. Others say they are just violent and sadistic criminals. NO! They are EVIL. They prey on and terrorize innocent men, women, and children for pleasure and self-gratification.

A DOJ report estimates that **pornographers have recorded (video) the abuse of more than one million children in the United States alone.**

CHAPTER 4: STATISTICS AND NUMBERS TO THINK ABOUT

One million children! Supposedly there is an increasing trend towards younger victims and greater brutality. (These are obviously investigative statistics, reports, and possibly video recordings that have been seized or seen on the Internet.)

An investigator with the federal Internet Crimes Against Children Task Force stated the following: "These guys are raping infants and toddlers. You can hear the child crying, pleading for help in the video. It is horrendous." Horrible! Our government must do more to stop these savage crimes. We must do more.

So, here is another figure: an estimated **one million children are the victims of child pornographers**. Does this include forced prostitution above and beyond the reported one hundred thousand figures? It is very likely. Does forced pornography and prostitution involve young and older adults who were kidnapped? It is very likely.

Another official report states that approximately **1.6 million children are sexually assaulted every year**. Here are some more shocking statistics: An estimated one out of four girls will be sexually molested by age eighteen, while one out of six boys will be sexually molested by age eighteen. I have seen another report that claims one out of five girls and one out of ten boys will be sexually assaulted. Either figure is far too outrageous to contemplate.

Again, whatever discrepancies there are in these statistics and numbers, the bottom line is we have an enormous and very deadly problem here in the United States when it comes to protecting our nation's children, teenagers, and adults.

Take the case of **Dr. Early Bradley**, a fifty-eight-year-old Delaware pediatrician. In 2011, Dr. Bradley was convicted and sentenced for molesting or raping eighty-five young girls and one boy. The actual number was estimated to be at least one hundred children, to include infants. Dr. Bradley recorded most of his assaults.

We all know that sexual abuses against children, both female and male, have been committed by family members and other relatives, friends and neighbors, members of the clergy, school teachers, day care and assisted living providers, doctors and other medical personnel, and complete strangers. The point here is that many of these sexual assaults result in traumatized children. Many victims are murdered and many of the bodies are forever hidden. Many victims are murder for pleasure and some are murdered to prevent them from becoming witnesses.

Where were the parents when this was happening? I guess they were in the waiting room. These parents, or guardians, should have been in the examination room with their child. Parents are responsible for their children's safety. How much simpler can that be? Watch your children! Educate your children and talk to them.

Now, when you complete your Individual Protection Packet and Biographical Form, you will understand why you should list different categories of associates, to include family members, school officials, coworkers, day-care sitters, medical professionals, friends, possible enemies, etc. These are people and investigative leads the police or detectives will want to know of and to pursue—*quickly*.

Missing Adults

Missing adults is every bit as serious as missing children. I think by now the issue is understood. Remember, **Let's Bring Them Home (LBTH)** is a national organization that can assist you with reporting and finding a missing loved one. They provide other support to victims and their families. After you have researched their website, contact LBTH and find out how you can support this organization as well.

Some of you may have heard of the National Center for Missing Adults (NCMA). Beginning in 2006, NCMA began experiencing funding cuts by Congress, and in 2009, Congress suddenly cut off all funding without any explanation. NCMA was later absorbed by LBTH. What happened here?

CHAPTER 4: STATISTICS AND NUMBERS TO THINK ABOUT

The LBTH website is linked to the RTI International website, where you can learn more about forensic science education as it relates to missing persons. The website also includes investigative strategies for current and cold cases. There are also training resources for law enforcement and information on fundraising and how you can become a political advocate.

Remember, the burden not only lies with our government and law enforcement—it is up to YOU as well! Parents and spouses need to step up to the plate. Businesses and organizations need to do their part, especially our schools and colleges. We as the people need to take steps to protect ourselves and our loved ones. Get started today.

Chapter 5

BECOME AN ADVOCATE FOR MISSING PERSONS

Okay, hopefully by now you are a concerned believer in the seriousness of this national problem. Over the past few years, I have been talking to people about this problem and the importance of the Individual Protection Packets. Not too many people seem concerned. Why? This is one reason I took the time to write this book.

Think about those figures. In a modern and civilized country of over three hundred million people, and in this era of technology and intelligence, one person is reported missing every thirty-two seconds, and most of them are children. Over 684,000 children are kidnapped every day. There are supposedly over 102,000 children and teenagers still missing. An estimated one million children are the victims of sexual abuse and child pornographers. We are not even discussing those adults aged eighteen and older.

Our great nation's missing persons epidemic is for some unexplainable reason very low on our government's radar screen—and is somewhat ignored by us as well, as individuals and parents. Not to mention the media. Why aren't we as parents and spouses doing more? We can decrease these numbers and these horrible odds with just a little effort. It doesn't take much. Please find the time to complete a protection packet on each of your loved ones. Take other steps to protect them.

Why is that it our media publicizes a few sensational cases or tosses us a few short news bites in the evening broadcast? Every newspaper in America should carry an insert informing us of recently missing persons in our area and nationwide. Every local news show on major radio and television stations should have a daily segment on missing persons. Not just a quick news bite, but a special segment that is well publicized and attracts listener and viewer attention.

Our investigative journalists and media owners should be focusing on this deadly epidemic here in the United States, as should our politicians. Instead, our media continues to focuses on politics, trivial Hollywood scandals, and other sensational news stories.

Remember the weekly episode *America's Most Wanted* with host John Walsh? John Walsh was the father of Adam Walsh, the six-year old boy who was kidnapped at a department store in Florida. Little Adam was later found murdered and decapitated. This tragic incident lead to the *Code Adam* program that now enables public businesses to take action when a child turns up missing at a mall or some other commercial location.

America's Most Wanted, a true reality crime show, lasted over twenty-three years and ended in 2011 due to the high cost of production. AMW was actually cancelled for one month in 1996 for the same reason. Money! Approximately **1,154 murderous fugitives were captured due to this show.** That averages out to over fifty murderers being taken off our streets and out of society each year. Thank you Mr. Walsh for all of your assistance to our families.

How many intelligent and decent people would be willing to watch a reality show that helps locate missing persons and save lives? Imagine if there was a *daily* television show dedicated to missing persons and the victims of possible kidnappings. Nothing elaborate, just a one-hour show describing recent events along with pictures and descriptions of both the victims and any suspects.

Next, our government could offer a national reward for each missing person. The cost of this reward could be offset by private donations offered by the family and supporters. Let's just pick an amount and say a $20,000 reward (or more). Isn't an innocent life worth that much money? It will cost the police five or ten times that amount to launch and conduct a proper investigation.

Now millions of people nationwide would be aware of these daily missing reports and some would have a monetary incentive to become involved. If viewers knew they could possibly receive $20,000 (or more) for helping to find a missing person, it is a sure bet more people will be watching and notifying the police. This would include the average citizen in cities and counties. This would include truckers and other drivers out on the interstates, highways, and streets. It would include private investigators, bounty hunters, bail bondsmen, and others who might make more of an effort if there was a monetary award. Imagine if every citizen knew they could potentially earn $20,000 for reporting something suspicious.

Can the government support such a costly national program? Absolutely! Should the government be involved in an enormous and elaborate program to recover missing children and save lives? Without a doubt! As explained earlier, our federal and state governments have both a legal and a moral obligation to protect us from harm. We also talked about new and innovative efforts.

How would this costly media effort be funded? To start with, advertisers and sponsors would gladly support this cause. Philanthropists and private donors would surely contribute to this effort. The federal and state governments should provide financial support as well. The newspapers, radio, and television stations could support this effort by reducing their production costs. It can be done.

As mentioned above, our federal government spends billions of taxpayer dollars every year on foreign aid, pork barrel, and wasteful earmarks. Not to mention research on anything from the behavioral habits of animals and insects to climate change control research.

Remember the superconducting super collider project? Over $12 billion was wasted before the government wised up and pulled the plug. Did they simply wise up or was something else going on? How about the Bridge to Nowhere? This earmark would have cost taxpayers over $200 million before it was stopped. The recent Cash-for-Clunkers program allegedly cost taxpayers $3 billion.

Okay, how about the $880 billion recently given to irresponsible financial institutions and other big businesses to supposedly bail them out of debt, with the true figure being as much as $16 trillion? These are just a few examples out of wasteful programs for which our government has spent trillions of dollars. A few years ago the White House reported that over $90 billion had been spent on programs deemed "ineffective, marginally adequate, or operating under a flawed purpose or design." This latter figure is obviously much higher than $90 billion.

In 2003, the federal government reported that over $25 billion was missing from the treasury, and for which there was no accounting. How much money has been reported as simply missing from the treasury since 2003? Our government has strict accounting principles and thousands of auditors. How does this happen?

A national missing-persons program can be funded for a fraction of the wasteful spending by our government. A national program should be funded considering the seriousness of this brutal and deadly epidemic. Such a program can and should be funded to prevent the inhuman torture, rape, and murder of innocent children and adults. Our government needs to do more to stop the commercial exploitation of child pornography and prostitution. Which is a more important, protecting foreign citizen in other countries or protecting American citizens here at home?

CHAPTER 5: BECOME AN ADVOCATE FOR MISSING PERSONS

Between the federal and state governments, philanthropists, and private donors, our nation can in fact afford a sophisticated nationwide missing-persons program. The federal and state governments need to step up to the plate and become more involved in curtailing this deadly epidemic. It needs to be a national priority.

Bottom line: With a little extra funding and effort by the federal and state governments, as well as individuals and parents, we might be able to slash these missing-person numbers by 50 or 75 percent.

Imagine if together we could save thousands of children and adults every year from being savagely beaten and brutally murdered. Imagine if we could prevent the heart-wrenching agony a family must suffer when such a tragedy happens to one of their loved ones. It's possible!

Would you like to become an advocate for missing children? **Talk to both your congressional and state representatives about this deadly epidemic.** I will tell you how. At the federal level you only have five people to contact: the President, your two US senators and your district representative in the US House of Representatives. Then contact your district representatives in the state General Assembly. Don't forget to contact your governor and mayor as well. Visit the LBTH website for some ideas on this contacting and recruiting you government representatives to do more.

Write each representative a personal letter or send them an e-mail. Mail them a copy of this book. They will appreciate the gesture. Follow up your correspondence with a scheduled telephone call. In your letter or e-mail give them all your contact information and tell them you will call their office in sixty days for a response. Ask them to provide you with a point of contact in their office.

Better yet, schedule a meeting with your representatives at one of their home offices in your state. This will have to be scheduled several months in advance. You can make this effort more effective by forming a small group.

How do you find the names and contact information for all your federal and state representatives? Google **"Congress.org**." Enter your zip code in the section titled "Get Involved." In the blink of an eye you will have all their names, office addresses, telephone numbers, and e-mail addresses.

While on Congress.org you can read a short biography of each of your representatives and learn what national and state bills (legislation) they sponsor and support. You are paying their salary and the salary and overhead of their staff. Find out what they are doing for you.

Some political districts cross over the standard five-digit zip code, so you may have to enter the additional four digits for your full nine digit zip code, e.g., 27529-*7943*. If you don't know the additional four digits at the end of your regular zip code, the website will help you along.

Simply click on any name and you will receive an information report on that representative, whether federal or state. One of the several tabs on that information report will provide you with all their contact information. You can even read a small biographical summary of each of your *elected* members. On that "Bio Sheet" will be a link to their official website for even more information.

Would you like to know more about your federal and state representatives' voting records and what committees they serve on? Sign up on Congress.org and receive a newsletter bulletin. You will learn how they vote on certain legislative bills and a little about the bills themselves.

You may also want to start talking to your governor, mayor, city or county manager, and local council members. Contact your local police department or sheriff's office. Find out how much they know about this deadly epidemic and ask what they are doing to protect you and your family. Know that most sheriffs are elected officials as well. Your elected officials work for *you*. They work for us—the American people.

CHAPTER 5: BECOME AN ADVOCATE FOR MISSING PERSONS

Here is another suggestion. Contact the owners and chief executive officers (CEOs) for the local newspapers and radio and television stations in your area, and find out how much they know about this national and local topic. What are they willing to do to help? This will take some research. If you have the knowledge and a written plan, you can be successful in bringing more attention to this serious problem. If you are part of a small working group, your chances of success will increase. Divide up the responsibilities within the group and make it easier. Not everyone has the time and resources to tackle this worthy cause. Just do what you can to help.

Before reading this book, were you aware of these numbers and how serious this problem really is right here in America? Like I said, this is a deadly epidemic which is very low on everyone's radar screen. Let's put it on the front page and on our front burner.

Let's start by exposing and confronting the matter. As disturbing as it may be, let's start by learning more about this deadly problem (awareness) and then figure out how to protect ourselves and our loved ones (prevention). It is time for each and every one of us to produce a *personal and home security plan*. It is a family effort. This plan will include workplaces and schools. It will even help protect us when we are on trips and vacations.

We, as individuals, spend thousands of dollars every year on "**health care**" for ourselves and our families; for example, medical insurance, prescription drugs, and over-the-counter medicines and supplies. Look what we spend on dental braces and for cosmetic surgery.

Every year we spend thousands more on "**personal care**" and luxuries we really don't need, such as expensive clothes and jewelry, toys and electronic gadgets, lavish entertainment, and vacations. We spend a lot of our money on nice cars, trucks, motorcycles, and boats.

Let's spend some of that money on "**life care**." It is really not that expensive to protect yourself.

Back to the bad guys. Sometimes these violent offenders continue to elude authorities or escape justice through legal technicalities. They are sometimes caught and released back into society to continue preying on innocent people.

Many liberal lawyers and judges actually believe these violent criminals and sex deviants can be rehabilitated. This has been an ongoing controversy for many years, and again, we do not hear much from the media about these judicial shortcomings and consequences. We do not hear much from our local, state, and federal governments about these failures.

Take the case of **Michael Woodmansee** who was convicted in 1983 for the murder of five-year-old Jason Foreman. Woodmansee lured little Jason into his home, where he murdered and allegedly cannibalized the poor boy. He was caught only after he tried to lure a second young boy into his home. Woodmansee was eventually convicted and sentenced to forty years in prison.

This monster was sentence to only forty years in jail after savagely murdering and cannibalizing an innocent child. He was released in the year 2011 after serving only twenty-nine years. Why was he released eleven years early after receiving a ridiculous sentence of only forty years? He was released from prison for good behavior.

Many times these monsters are released because they are supposedly rehabilitated. Rehabilitated! How to you rehabilitate a monster?

Let's talk **criminal recidivism**. These are the cases of repeat and habitual offenders who are in and out of prison. They are given second chances at freedom in an innocent society. We are not going to consider recidivism as it relates to drug users, thieves, or other criminals.

Let's just talk about *criminal recidivism* as it relates to criminal psychopathy. This term applies to an offender has some form of a diagnosed psychosis and was involved in extreme acts of intentional violence or sexual crimes.

CHAPTER 5: BECOME AN ADVOCATE FOR MISSING PERSONS

There have been numerous studies on violent criminal/psychopathy recidivism and rehabilitation. Some of the studies and statistics claim that around 80 percent of these violent criminals repeat their crimes after being released from prison. Some argue the numbers are much lower and some argue they are higher, but everyone just argues their opinions that are based on manipulated statistics. Who cares about the opinions of these so-called pundits and academic intellectuals?

There should not be any constitutional, legal, or moral rights afforded to any terrorist or criminal after they have been convicted of extreme acts of violence and brutality; and that includes sexual crimes. A criminal should never be freed once they are convicted of knowingly and intentionally taking the life of an innocent person in cold blood. In addition, if they are arrested and charged with either a violent or sexual crime, they should have no right to bond or bail while awaiting trial.

This includes their incarceration. Those found to be temporally insane should never be released for a heinous crime. They certainly should not be released based on good behavior or prison overcrowding. They should not receive any luxuries or comfort while in prison. Most inmates receive better living conditions than most of our military troops in combat zones. They receive expensive medical care that is not always available to our law-abiding citizens. They live better than most poor families and certainly the homeless.

In fact, medical care for prisoners is a large part of every state budget, costing taxpayers billions of dollars every year. Forget about this human rights crap when it comes to serial killers and sadistic rapists and torturers. They do not need expensive dental care. They do not deserve expensive medical care. If someone is on "death row", why are we giving them cancer and other treatment to keep them alive? Keep in mind, I am talking about people who have committed atrocities, not a murder of passion or negligence.

Our government and media should be more active and vocal about this horrific and deadly epidemic. Our courts and legal system should be harsher. It's ludicrous to even think most of these extremely violent animals and monsters can be rehabilitated and deserve another chance. It is absurd and offensive to a victim's family to release a brutal killer from prison based on good behavior or overcrowding. It is irrational to release a suspected killer on bond to simply ensure his rights are protected.

Over the past few years, our federal government even argued that sadistic terrorists captured overseas should be brought to this country to protect their rights and ensure a fair trial. I have encountered some of these terrorists. They are not human beings. They are monsters who savagely maim and murder innocent people for excitement and pleasure. Why should they be brought to the United States to protect their rights and have a fair trial? This was *our* US Attorney General making this argument! What is wrong with our government? Why wasn't this Attorney General fired for even making such a declaration?

Oops—back on track. What about the criminally insane and less significant psychiatric defenses. Crazy! Despite what some doctors may claim, I believe some of these severe psychopaths have some level of understanding when it comes to knowing right from wrong, and that they understand the consequences of their actions, but the bottom line is they only care about themselves and their sadistic cravings. They know what they did was wrong, but they have little or no feelings or remorse towards their victims or family.

The scariest part is they can function normally with and around other people. They marry and have children. They hold jobs and socialize with others. But then, all of the sudden, they are declared criminally insane, and that is a legitimate defense for being released later and escaping justice. What's even scarier is the overly liberal lawyers and judges who give them that second and third chance. When doctors declare a monster is criminally insane and not responsible for his actions, that is hogwash. Either way, they should never be released back into society.

What do you think about becoming an advocate for missing persons? In addition to learning how to protect yourself and your loved ones, are you

CHAPTER 5: BECOME AN ADVOCATE FOR MISSING PERSONS

willing to do more? Start by contacting the national support organizations and make a private donation or volunteer to help. In fact, *a portion of the proceeds from this book will be given to these support organizations.* So, you are already helping.

Next, contact your congressional and state legislators and motivate them as well. In fact, demand they become involved. After all they are supposed to serve us—their constituents and the American people. There are other things you can do, and they start with your neighborhood and community.

Do you have a *neighborhood watch* program? Volunteer to help or start one yourself. Too much to deal with or tackle? Get together with a few neighbors and agree to watch one another's homes. Just do whatever you can. This is another reason for using lights around your home and property at night. It allows the neighbor across the street keep an eye on your home.

Chapter 6

PERSONAL AWARENESS AND PREVENTION

Do you lock your doors and windows at night and close the curtains? If so, why? Pause for a several seconds and answer that question.

When your children go out somewhere, do you warn them to be careful and then worry a little bit the rest of the evening? Again, pause and think about the answers.

When you walk or drive through a dark or unsafe part of town, are you a little nervous? Do you find yourself looking around or over your shoulder? Do you sometimes feel you are being followed? Do you find yourself being a little more cautious or nervous under these circumstances? If so, you are being smart. Your instincts are in place. Congratulations!

In the military and law enforcement we say, *"Fear is good."* Fear keeps us alert and causes us to undertake certain precautions. Fear doesn't necessarily have to project a bad connotation. Yes, fear is good and it is normal. It's a natural survival instinct. It just needs to be understood and controlled. You don't want to become paranoid or obsessed about safety and security, but you do want to be smart and *vigilant*. That's a great word—vigilant! To be observant and cautious.

I remember one morning driving by an obviously pregnant lady walking along a busy interstate. I had just passed her car broken down on the side of the highway. I stopped and offered her a ride, but she refused to get in the car. I showed her my badge. No good. I then radioed communications and had them dispatch a wrecker. She was thankful, but still would not get in the car to sit down.

She explained that her husband told her never to get in a car with a stranger no matter what the problem. Good advice! She was being smart and exercising caution despite her uncomfortable situation of pregnancy, being late for work, and walking along a highway. That was a strong lady. All sorts of murders and violent assaults have been committed by police impersonators.

One evening my wife was out and she spotted a car following her. She took a few *evasive maneuvers* (extra turns) and the car continued to follow her. The driver then turned on a dashboard blue light as he pulled closer behind her. If the other car was a police vehicle, she couldn't tell. It wasn't marked and she too knew to be weary of such vehicles/drivers.

My wife proceeded to a well-lit gas station. A uniformed officer got out of his car and approached her. He was a little irritated she didn't stop right away, but after she explained she was doing what she was taught by her husband, he understood. Or maybe he was impressed she listened. Ha! *(No, you didn't just say that?)* Just kidding. She was being cautious—she was being smart! Another strong lady.

Crucial advice: Kidnappers and murderers have been known to pose as police officers and use dashboard-mounted lights to stop unsuspecting drivers. They have also been known to use this ruse at homes as well.

If an unmarked vehicle stops you and the driver is *not* wearing a uniform (as he approaches your car), I advise you to leave and drive to the nearest

CHAPTER 6: PERSONAL AWARENESS AND PREVENTION

location that is well lit and where there are other people. Drive the speed limit and drive carefully. Don't panic. As you are driving, call 911 and advise them of the situation. Police officers and dispatchers are aware of this precaution.

A suspicious stop will usually involve a male using a dashboard light (as opposed to rooftop or grill lights), wearing plain clothes, or wearing only a police jacket (windbreaker). Sometimes these imposters will strap on a utility belt that makes them look more like a cop. They will turn on their vehicle's bright lights so you cannot see very well. They might shine their flashlight in your eyes or in your mirror to blind you. Wow! This book is littered with good advice.

If you are stopped by an unmarked car for no apparent reason and the driver gets out wearing a full uniform, you still want to be cautious. What does your gut feeling tell you? Lock your door, crack your window about three inches, and keep the car running, but put it in *park*. If it is nighttime, turn on your overhead light. Plant your foot firmly on the brake pedal and keep it there. Be prepared to place your car in gear and leave if anything out of the ordinary occurs.

If you feel something is really suspicious, you may want to call 911. Tell them you have just been pulled over by an unmarked car and the driver appears to be a cop, but that you are not sure. Try to describe your location and your car. Again, the dispatcher should be able to determine your location. The cop may hear you speaking to the dispatcher and if he is legitimate he will not be upset.

Okay, back to a good *security plan*. Make a checklist of what you want to do. When you devise your plan, set goals and time limits; for example, "I will complete the Individual Protection Packet(s) within two weeks." "I will call three companies and get estimates for an alarm system by the end of the month."

A plan is a map showing you a clear path you can follow through an unfamiliar forest. A plan with both short-term and long-term goals helps you achieve success and it helps those who tend to procrastinate or get sidetracked.

A security plan is absolutely necessary for safety and survival. Don't rely on luck. Producing a good security plan for yourself and your family is not a time to procrastinate or take shortcuts. Security is about your safety and the safety of others who depend on you—those you care about and love.

You have probably heard this age old adage, "An ounce of prevention is worth a pound of cure." We all know to be careful, but we must all *know* and learn *how* to be careful. By reading this book and completing your own research, you have taken the first step—*awareness*. By completing the Individual Protection Packets/Biographical Forms on each of your loved ones and following any of the security recommendations below, you have taken the second step—*prevention*.

You are about to receive some good advice and tips on personal and family security. Use this information however you decide, but do *something*. Be smart and be proactive! Be vigilant!

By learning and taking decisive action you will decrease the odds that a predator will choose to target you, a family member, or your home. You will increase your odds of being safe and secure. If your children or loved ones suddenly disappear, you will drastically increase the odds they will be found or rescued as quickly as possible. Don't rely on luck or wishful thinking. Rely on yourself. Rely on your efforts and your brain. Be realistic about life and the criminal threat that is all around you.

Keep in mind that an abduction, or kidnapping, can occur as a result of *force* or *deception*. Even those who think they are in control of a situation or being cautious can easily fall victim to violent criminals and sexual predators—who are often very shrewd and calculating. Even if you are smart enough to outthink a kidnapper, you may not be physically strong enough to prevent being overwhelmed by sheer swiftness and force.

CHAPTER 6: PERSONAL AWARENESS AND PREVENTION

Men often lose a physical struggle against these attackers, but women and children are usually more susceptible to physical dominance. These predators are like hawks; they will swoop down from nowhere and snatch you away. Many of these criminals have tools readily available for subduing and silencing their victims; and they practice their take-down techniques.

These attack tools include guns and knives, stun devices (Tasers), or blackjacks and batons. Attackers may even use mace, but that can backfire on them. Restraints will usually include flex-cuffs (plastic), handcuffs (metal), duct tape, rope, and/or hoods. Many of the criminals will have masks and gloves (leather or latex). If you know someone with these items, your antennas should be tingling.

Some of these deviants suffer from mild or severe "antisocial personality disorders," and many suffer some level of severe and deadly "psychosis." You never know where you will cross paths with one of these psychopaths, and you will probably not recognize them until it is too late.

The **Internet** and **dating services** make this possibility of stalking and an attack even more likely. The Internet and dating services can be a hunting environment for many of these animals. Using the Internet and dating services can be perfectly safe if you use common sense and exercise certain precautions.

Here is some good advice. I will elaborate in Chapter 5. These are several steps you need to seriously consider as part of your new security plan:

Starting right now! Complete an Individual Protection Packet on yourself and each of your loved ones. This includes the Biographical Form. Keep it with you at all times so you can hand it to the police in the event someone turns up missing. Don't forget to keep it updated. This should be your number-one step to complete.

Make it a new rule: always check in with someone wherever you go. If you go to several locations, check in each step of the way. Let someone know who you are with and the name of the location. The other person needs to remember this information and the times. Write it down. Parents, this is not a time for Twenty-One Questions—just be glad they are calling.

Come up with a personal and family security plan. Sit down as a family and discuss this plan. **Communicate!**

Take *security measures* at home, work, and school. First, buy an alarm system, and hopefully a "monitoring" service, for your home. These systems are no longer expensive and easy to install. You need an alarm system in your car as well, or at least a panic alarm. Second, start leaving your outside lights on all night. Wherever there are doors and windows, there should be light.

Buy one or more personal GPS tracking devices for your children and spouse. You can monitor their whereabouts from your cell phone or your computer using any street-map guide. You can even see how fast they are going. Think about that. If your child is in school or home and going fifty-five miles per hour, something may be wrong. Or, you have a very talented child.

DO NOT meet with strangers alone, especially when it involves the Internet and online dating services. If you can't have someone with you, always make sure someone knows where you are and what you are doing. Again, all it takes is a simple phone call or text message. In fact, snap a picture of your new acquaintance and send that to someone in a text message. You can be obvious about doing this and turn it into a joke. If your date is offended, it is a warning this person is a potential attacker—or a jerk. A good person will not think anything about this and will have nothing to hide.

DO NOT provide strangers with *personal information*, such as your full name, home address, telephone numbers, date-of-birth (DOB), and/or social security number. With just some of this information, a criminal can find the rest on the Internet and through public record searches. *Social networks* such as Facebook, My Space, dating services, etc. can be hunting grounds for predators. This also applies to *identity theft*. Please, go on

CHAPTER 6: PERSONAL AWARENESS AND PREVENTION

your social profiles and remove your DOB, phone numbers, and address. Think about this! If someone you know needs this personal information, then let them ask and give it to them in private.

DO NOT open your door to strangers and do not invite them into your home. Never ever let your *children* answer the door alone. If a stranger unexpectedly rings your doorbell, call a neighbor, friend, or relative. Just holding the phone in your hand with someone on the other end may save your life. If the stranger is in fact a criminal or potential attacker, he may be hesitant to attack. You can simply hold the telephone receiver in your hand with no one on the other end and pretend someone is on the other line. Make sure the person at your door sees the phone and you can even speak, or pretend to speak, to someone. However, it is suggested to have a live body on the other end.

Avoid encounters and confrontations with strangers in secluded and dark areas. Be aware of your surroundings. Keep your head and eyes moving. Walk quickly and with confidence. Have your remote control key FOB or something in your hands to protect yourself. If a stranger appears to be deliberately walking in your direction, attract someone's attention by pushing the panic button. You can also yell or run. You can be embarrassed and apologize later. If you don't have a car FOB with a panic button, carry a whistle or canned air horn in your hand. I believe in stun guns (Taser) and mace.

Be aware of someone following you in your car. It is a very common tactic used by rapists and serial killers. If you identify a car possibly following you, then make a few extra turns and see if they continue to follow. Then call the police. Don't go home if they are following you. Proceed to a well-lit location with some people around. If you can safely get a description of the car, license plate, and driver, even better. Just be careful, but let's not be afraid to fight back. I had rather die fighting than to die cowering.

I'm a big believer in personal defense. You may want to consider purchasing a weapon of some sort. It can be a shotgun, handgun, stun gun, or mace.

When you purchase something like this, you need professional training on proper use, to include safety. Not only for yourself, but for your entire family, to include children. Children are not stupid or unaware, but they are curious. They should be properly educated about any weapons you keep in the house.

I could speak volumes on weapons, but you will either approve or reject their use. Like I said, if you purchase a weapon, make sure you get *professional training*. Make sure the weapons are stored in a safe place where they cannot be accessed by children and others. Last, make sure you fully understand the *laws* governing the possession and use of certain weapons. More information will be provided on all these suggestions.

Vicious assaults are undeniable and happen every minute of the day. Knowing this, you should closely monitor your children's activities: who they associate with, where they go, when they are on the Internet, etc. The same goes for adults. As family members we need to keep one another informed. Some parents rely on trust. If you know your child follows directions and always does the right thing, then you are very fortunate. Many children are very honest in their interactions with their parents and follow rules. Awesome! However, you still need to know where they are and who they are with.

I was pleasantly surprised when my physical therapist said she always called her mother or father when she went somewhere and kept them posted along the way. She is teaching her children the same thing.

It takes less than a minute to kidnap a child or adult—sometimes just seconds. People need to be free and allowed to enjoy life, but we can learn how to be aware of our surroundings and take certain precautions. Remember the story about the little girl in Walmart? Becoming a *hard target* as opposed to a *soft target* will increase your odds of staying alive and going unharmed. Buying and using inexpensive security devices will help. Be prepared! Become a hard target!

CHAPTER 6: PERSONAL AWARENESS AND PREVENTION

People often marvel at the seemingly dangerous tactics employed by military personnel and SWAT teams, even in training. It is all about knowledge, proper techniques, repetitive training, and safety. There is no magic to what they do.

These professionals pull off some extremely dangerous stunts and are safer than the rest of us. Why? Because they are knowledgeable, prepared, and trained. Training is so important, even if it only involves discussions and mental rehearsals. Actual hands-on training and rehearsals work better. It is time for us to learn more about this topic, and we must sit down with our loved ones and prepare them. It is time for us to take the necessary precautions and start training and rehearsing ourselves.

Some so-called experts say the first twenty-four or forty-eight hours, or even seventy-two hours, is the crucial period during which to find a missing person. Nonsense! They need to be found in the first *few* hours. With this very short time constraint, don't you think it would be best to provide the police and investigators with all the crucial information they need to begin their *initial search and investigation*? Don't you think it would be best to have everything together and be able to hand it over at once?

That's the importance of the Individual Protection Packet and the Biographical Form. You can provide this electronic file cabinet to the police and within minutes they have everything they need to initiate a successful search, investigation, and rescue. They will have answers to all the questions and clues they need to pursue. Where is this crucial information? Most of it will be on a small and secure USB flash (thumb) drive you can carry with you. You can leave a copy at work, home, in your car, or with a trusted relative or friend.

Another statistic states it can take law enforcement up to two hours to collect all the necessary information they need to initiate their preliminary search and investigation. Wooooah! The first few hours! Isn't that the crucial time frame in which to *find* a loved one? That's two hours wasted, and even then, certain crucial questions may not have been asked or answered until later—even days later. Simply give the police officer or detective your USB thumb drive with your Individual Protection Packet(s) and they will have what they need in a few minutes, versus two hours or the next few days.

What makes up your Individual Protection Packet (IPP)? The Biographical Form provides *investigative leads.* Investigative leads are crucial information and clues police and investigators need to know right away and act upon. The Biographical Form answers every question they will ask you, and some that they may forget to ask. Can a police officer or detective forget to ask an important question? Of course! We are all human. We all make mistakes or forget things. I call them brain infarctions. (Did I clean up that word or what?) You can carry most of this information with you at all times. It's simple to prepare and easy to carry.

Let's clarify some important terms and meanings used by police officers and investigators. Why do you need to know this? You really don't. Just be familiar with the terms, so you can more effectively interact with the people in this particular profession. Knowledge! Understanding!

Law Enforcement (LE) includes your local police departments, county sheriff's office, and state or highway police. *Law Enforcement Officers* (LEOs) include uniform officers who initially respond and plainclothes detectives who conduct follow-up investigations. *Detectives* are also known as *inspectors* and *investigators.* If a detective does not show up on the scene, there is already both a problem and delay. You need a detective who is trained and capable of conducting a quick but thorough investigation. Remember: LE, LEO, and detectives.

Crucial advice: If you felt the need to make a missing-person report, then the matter *is* in fact serious. This is not a guessing game. You need a trained and skilled detective at the scene to initiate the investigation. If a uniformed police officer responds first, there had better be a detective in route.

CHAPTER 6: PERSONAL AWARENESS AND PREVENTION

Very close relatives of mine were recently robbed. One robbery involved a break-in of a car parked at her apartment complex, and the other was an in-house theft of valuable jewelry.

In the first case, one evening, several cars were broken into at a rather large apartment complex. My daughter left a small wallet in the car and was able to determine the next morning that someone used her credit card at a nearby restaurant for breakfast. After calling the restaurant she determined they had security cameras that would have recorded the person using the stolen credit card. This information was given to the police, but a LEO or detective never followed up on this crucial *investigative lead,* despite the fact they knew the incident involved several other cars. I was so irritated I poked myself in the eye to make the anger go away.

My in-laws discovered that a box of jewelry was taken from their bedroom closet. Only the expensive jewelry was taken, with the costume jewelry being left behind. Does that spell S-M-A-R-T thief? A uniformed LEO responded the following day and the officer attempted to take fingerprints. The suspects were cleaning ladies who happened to all be in the *same bedroom together for a lengthy period.* This was, of course, not normal; they should not have all been in the same room for an hour. Their routine was to split up and clean the house, and clean one room or usually two in fifteen to twenty minutes. When something does not seem right, it probably isn't! Find out. Curiosity didn't kill the cat. It was a car the cat didn't see.

A detective did not get involved until several weeks later. After more than a month had passed by, none of the witnesses and suspects had been properly interviewed. Some of the jewelry was very expensive and other pieces were also sentimental.

Too late! Uniformed LEOs are not trained investigators. Detectives have dozens of cases and cannot pursue every case and every lead to its fullest potential. Time is of the essence in any crime, especially missing-persons crimes. That's the point of these two stories.

Crucial advice (repeated): A missing-person report is a *very* serious matter and warrants immediate action by trained and skilled police investigators. Hire a private investigator if *you* feel it is necessary.

Here is some advice: do *not* leave valuable items in your car and do not leave them in plain sight in your house where they can be seen through the windows. If a thief is "casing" the parking lot or driveways and spots any valuable items in plain view, they will smash your window to get the money or valuables. When I say "money" this includes small change, even a one-dollar bill. If they see even a small amount, they will think there is more to find.

Same goes for your house. If a thief peeks through the windows and see your wallet, purse, cell phone, and other small valuable items in plain view, they may commit a smash and grab. It will happen so fast they will be gone before you can fully wake up and get out of bed.

Speaking of peeping Toms, people outside in the dark can clearly see everything inside a house, even with just a little inside lightening. Outside lights make viewing inside the house less clear, and exposes Tom. You also need to use blinds and drapes—in the daytime as well.

Do *not* think you can simply hide valuable items from burglars who enter your home, either invited or uninvited. Watch those who are in your home even if you have to follow them around. When cleaners and repairmen are in our homes, for hours, we tend to forget about them. Buy a good, heavy safe that cannot be easily moved. Secure it to the floor with a steel cable and eyebolt if necessary. Keep your valuables in that safe. Buy a small-motion alarm and hook it to the safe. If someone tries to remove the device or move the safe, an alarm will go off.

You can purchase a safe with the old-fashioned dial combination or one with an electronic number keypad. These safes even come with "electronic

CHAPTER 6: PERSONAL AWARENESS AND PREVENTION

biometric fingerprint scanners." All it takes is a swipe of your fingertip and the safe will open. You can program in several fingerprints from different family members. Can't get any easier than that. I recommend you purchase one that is fireproof as well. This will be a safe place to keep you passport, birth-certificates, vehicle title, last will and testament, and other valuable papers.

Let's get back to your law enforcement education. I'm not very good at keeping on track, but I already told you I'm not a professional writer. LE and LEO also include *federal authorities* such as *Special Agents* (criminal investigators) from the Federal Bureau of Investigation (FBI) and Homeland Security Investigations (HSI). Remember: Special Agents (criminal investigators) from the FBI and HSI.

There are also uniformed Customs and Border Protection (CBP) officers who are stationed at all our air, sea, and land borders. These uniformed inspectors are called CBP officers. CBP also includes *agents* from the US Border Patrol (USBP). These uniformed border patrol officers are "Border Patrol Agents" and they are not Special Agents—or trained criminal investigators. But they have special skills when it comes to illegal border crossings and smuggling. Some are even professional trackers. Remember: CBP officers and border patrol agents.

The Department of State has *Regional Security Officers* (RSOs) assigned to US embassies and consulates around the world. FBI, HSI, and CBP also have representatives working in US embassies worldwide. HSI special agents, CBP officers and border patrol agents all fall under the Department of Homeland Security. The Central Intelligence Agency (CIA) and our military branches have representatives and attaches at our embassies as well. Together, they make a force to be reckoned with. Remember: FBI, HSI, CBP, RSO, CIA, and military "*attaches.*" Sometimes the LE representatives are also called attaches.

There is a lot of LE support for *interstate* and *international* kidnappings. By the way, the FBI has jurisdiction (authority) when a kidnapping involves foreign, interstate travel, ransom, and other certain crimes. They are very experienced in these areas and have more manpower, money, and resources than most police departments. Getting the FBI involved may be difficult, but it can be done.

The same problem may occur with the special agents and officers from HSI, CBP, and RSOs, but they can get involved in a search and rescue as it relates to international matters, including the borders and foreign countries. These are good resources to be *aware* of, so learn more about these federal law enforcement and investigative agencies.

There are several national-level organizations that have been tasked by federal law to assist with missing children and adults. They include the **National Center for Missing and Exploited Children** (NCMEC) and **Let's Bring Them Home** (LBTH) for adults. You read about these organizations earlier.

Most states have their own missing children and adult programs. There are many other private organizations willing to assist you with locating missing children and adults, as well as with mentally coping with this tragedy. Four of them are the **Polly Klaas Foundation**, **Klaas Kids Foundation**, and the **Association of Missing and Exploited Children's Organization (AMECO), Child Quest International (CQI)**. There are more. Take a look at http://www.child-safety-for-parents.com. There is valuable information on protecting children and a section for different organizations.

A partner or family member can offer emotional support, but a *professional counselor* is trained to deal specifically with these incidents and the stress it can cause to a family and between spouses. Missing-children incidents have been known to destroy marriages over time. These organizations are described throughout this book and are listed in the back of this book. Please research all these organizations I have mentioned and others that I may have missed. Always seek professional counseling.

CHAPTER 6: PERSONAL AWARENESS AND PREVENTION

Crucial advice: If your loved ones turn up missing and you suspect foul play, contact the police immediately and then contact NCMEC or LBTH.

After speaking to the representatives at either organization, write down their name, contact information, and the "case number." Do *not* wait for the LEO or detective to contact NCMEC or LBTH. You do *not* need their permission to contact either support organization. Remember, this is *your* loved one.

However, let the LEO or detective know who you have contacted and provide them with your points of contact and case number. After you have met with the LEO and detectives, recontact NCMEC or LEBTH and give them the name of the detective handling your case, along with all contact information and case number. Both the LEO and the organizations need to coordinate and should be working together. Confirm this by *you* being involved.

This action may upset some LEO or detectives. It should not, and out of respect for my brothers in law enforcement I will not explain why they get upset. It's unprofessional and old-school. If you receive any negative feedback for your personal actions, remember it is *your* loved one. It is your right to ask questions and take action. However, at the same time, you want to ensure proper communication and coordination. You also want to avoid conflicts. You will be under enough stress should this tragedy strike. Teamwork, communications, and coordination is more effective than everyone going off independently in different directions with bad attitudes. That's counterproductive. When there is a group effort, I always say one person has to drive the car and the others can navigate. You can't have more than one set of hands and feet on the steering wheel and pedals.

I have also operated under the very old proverb and philosophy: "Two heads are better than one." Bureaucracies, territorial arguments, jurisdictional disputes, and egos are very detrimental to good law enforcement and solving crimes. Someone needs to poke these dinosaurs or egomaniacs in the eye. Like the Germans say, "Ich vill mit der finger gepoken."

As far as *state* missing-person organizations, in North Carolina you can call the Community United Effort (CUE) Center for Missing Persons, or CUE Center. There are also a few other private organizations that assist in searches. This is just one example. Learn more about *your* state LE agencies and private organizations. Write down all their telephone numbers and store them in your cell phone or home phone directory. Give these numbers to your day-care center and babysitter as well.

As we said, the first step is *awareness*. This means *knowledge*. Are you willing to take the time to start your own research? You need to, because learning what to do after the incident is simply too late. Do you put on your seat belt after the crash? Can you put on a reserve chute after your main parachute fails? Start learning more about missing and exploited *children*, as well as missing and exploited *adults*.

What is an exploited person? These are children, teenagers, and adults who are kidnapped for servitude (slavery), pornography, sexual gratification (pleasure), or prostitution. It is usually for commercial profit, i.e. money.

How do you force a child, teenager, or adult into pornography or prostitution? Some predators have a bizarre and extraordinary influence over their captives. In the beginning they can seem very charismatic. They can manipulate children and adults through favors (being nice) and fear (being mean), which includes threats against parents or other family members. Some force the cooperation of their victims through beatings and drugs. They know how to identify weaknesses and play on them. There have been numerous cases throughout America in which teenage girls have been involved in forced prostitution while going to school and living at home with their parents.

The FBI estimated that from 100,000 to 150,000 children and young women are trafficked in America today for sex and prostitution. They

CHAPTER 6: PERSONAL AWARENESS AND PREVENTION

range in age from nine to nineteen, with the average age being eleven. I have seen figures much higher. The figures on young women brought to the United States for sex slavery are even worse.

But, let's look at a few cases that involved the typical "girl next door." Google, "*MSNBC Today Shauna Newell*" and "*MSNBC Today Theresa Flores*." I could elaborate on these horrible and sad stories, but go online so you can read about their plights and watch the news videos. Apparently the parents had no idea what was happening and why their children weren't talking to them. Wow! You need to explain to your children that they can talk to you or someone else about sexual abuse.

Here are just a few of more cases that also involved kidnappings. You can Google these crimes as well. Research and read more about nineteen-year-old Patty Hurst, fourteen-year-old Elizabeth Smart, eleven-year-old Jaycee Dugard, twelve-year-old Polly Klaas, and ten-year-old Jeffrey Curley.

Patty Hurst, age nineteen, was a young adult who was kidnapped and held captive for over a year. She was coerced into committing bank robberies and other felony crimes with her captors. This case brought national attention to brainwashing (mind control) and the Stockholm Syndrome.

Elizabeth Smart, age fourteen, was a young girl kidnapped from her bedroom, which she shared with her sister at the time. Despite an extensive statewide search she was found nine months later living with her captors only eighteen miles from her home. During her captivity she was repeatedly raped. Her story is now a movie and a book. Her captors were husband and wife. Wow! Where was the wedding for those two monsters performed?

Jaycee Dugard, age eleven, was a young girl kidnapped while walking home from school. She was subdued when her captors used a stun gun (Taser), which Jaycee's stepfather witnessed. It happened just that fast. Jaycee was held by her captors for eighteen years in the same state where she lived. She was repeatedly raped and abused. Her abductors were another husband and wife team and their residence was searched for various reasons over the years. Yet authorities never discovered Jaycee was being held captive and living in the backyard in a tent.

Polly Klaas, age twelve, was kidnapped from her home during a slumber party with other children. She was taken right from her home at knife point, which was witnessed by some of the other children. Over the next two months more than four thousand people helped search for Polly. Her murderer was later captured. Polly's father, Marc Klaas, established the *Klaas Kids Foundation* in her memory and to help other victims. Please visit that website for excellent assistance and advice. The link, like most others, is in the back of the book.

Jeffrey Curley, age ten, was kidnapped in 1997 by two men, Salvatore Sicari and Charlie Jaynes. These two despicable animals raped and later murdered young Jeffrey Curley. Salvatore Sicari lived down the street from the Curley family and had his eye on Jeffrey. Salvatore Sicari and Charlie Jaynes were later arrested and convicted. As a side note, Salvatore's brother, Robert Sicari, was also convicted of raping a young boy in a separate incident. As most of us know, child molesters and rapists are often childhood victims themselves.

Salvatore Sicari and Charlie Jaynes claimed they were unduly influenced by pornography and the **North American Man/Boy Love Association** (NAMBLA). Curley's parents later sued NAMBLA for wrongful death, claiming NAMBLA influenced violent predatory behavior. Incredibly, the American Civil Liberties Union (ACLU) represented NAMBLA and was successful in having the lawsuit dismissed.

There are a lot of violent influences in our society, and when you have structured organizations like NAMBLA and the ACLU protecting the rights of pedophiles and other criminal deviants, parents must take extra precautions to protect their children. As parents and family members, we must be vigilant at all times. We must have each other's backs.

CHAPTER 6: PERSONAL AWARENESS AND PREVENTION

By the way, the ACLU is a powerful legal organization that represents some of our most notorious criminals under the auspice of defending *their* "legal rights," They have somehow convinced themselves to ignore the obvious rights of innocent and law-abiding victims. This is just my opinion. For the ACLU, it is not about right from wrong; morals or justice. To them it is probably about the legal challenge, the love of power, publicity, and the limelight. You decide.

I remember two legal cases in which the ACLU tried to destroy the Boy Scouts of America (BSA) because this "private organization" fired a gay scout leader and recognized God. I mention this not because of religion or sexual orientation. The ACLU not only sued the BSA, but they fought to stop the BSA from holding rallies on federal property. In many people's opinions, the ACLU used the legal system to harass and attempt to drive the BSA into financial hardships. The BSA eventually won both battles.

Crucial advice: First, parents (and guardians) must learn how to protect their children. Second, parents can and should teach their children what they need to know about the *other world* and what they should do to prevent being kidnapped or becoming the victim of criminal influences. Third, parents must teach their children what to do if they are kidnapped or put in harm's way.

Parents are directly and ultimately responsible for their children's safety and well-being. *You* are their parents, guardians, and disciplinarians first and foremost; and their friends second. Today's parents must get back to basic parenting. Stop blaming everyone else. Be ever loving, but be responsible. You will shape and mold your child for the future.

Mind control, also known as **brainwashing**, is very real and a threat that needs to be understood and countered. You just read several cases involving mind control.

There was another case in which **Shawn Hornbeck** was kidnapped at the age of eleven years while riding his bike. He was held captive for more than four years and was repeatedly tortured and raped by his captor. At the same time, young Shawn was allowed by his abductor (and rapist) to leave the apartment alone to ride his bicycle. Why didn't Shawn seek help? It's complicated. Shawn was eventually rescued after his abductor tried to kidnap another boy and was caught by the police.

Speaking of mind control and brainwashing, most of us recall the men, women, and children who took their lives at the instruction of Reverend Jim Jones of the People's Temple. The Reverend Jones influenced over nine hundred men, women, and children to commit mass suicide. That's mind control. That's a whole new issue, cults, and kidnappings. Learn more about cults and brainwashing. Learn where you can get professional and legal help when your loved one is an adult and has become a member of a cult.

Does all this really happen in the United States? You had better believe it. Read some of the *Dateline NBC* stories on sex slavery, date rapes, and child molesters. Watch some of the useful videos they produce online. Get your fingers to do the "Google."

What about protecting the elderly? Research the **National Center on Elder Abuse** (NCEA) website. Learn more about the **National Silver Alert Act** and **Silver Alerts** for missing adults, primarily the elderly. Do you have any idea how easy it is for a criminal to prey on the elderly who have diminished physical and mental capacities? Our elderly are also very vulnerable to con artists, who will steal every penny they have left in life.

Adults with Alzheimer's disease and dementia are known to wander away from home or assisted living facilities, as are children with autism. Later you will learn more about personal GPS safety devices and how they can help locate people.

You were told about the National Center for Missing and Exploited Children (NCMEC), and there is voluminous information on that website. A lot of that information can be applied to missing adults as well. But what about eighteen-year-olds who are no longer considered children?

CHAPTER 6: PERSONAL AWARENESS AND PREVENTION

Our law enforcement and government generally consider anyone "under" the age of eighteen years to be a child. Teenagers eighteen and nineteen years of age, are considered adults under our missing-persons program. That's insane and that is just flat wrong. If you talk to your legislators, please encourage them to change the law to include the ages eighteen and nineteen. Most eighteen and nineteen-year-olds are still living at home with Mom and Dad and going to school. You will read more about this.

Many of us know about **Amber Alerts**, which provide the public with emergency information on missing children. But do you know about the **Code Adam** alerts for businesses? How about **Net Smart**, **Cyber Tip Line**, and the **Child Victim Identification Program**? I just looked the other day and saw **InHope**— the International Association of Internet Hotlines.

These programs are related to missing persons and child pornography or exploitation. Read about these topics on the NCMEC website. There is a lot of material that can be downloaded or ordered by mail. Share this information with your entire family, no matter how unpleasant it may seem. NCMEC even has material on how to teach young children and teenagers, to include publications and video tapes.

Crucial advice: As the protector of your loved ones, know what your younger children, teenagers, and other loved ones are doing and with whom they associate. This includes the parents of their friends.

This is not an invasion of privacy; it is about responsibility and protection. It is about life and death. Both children and adults of any age can be as easily manipulated or exploited.

Do you know how many young girls and women are raped and murdered in their own homes or while on dates? Do you know about **date rapes**? What about **date-rape drugs**? Do you know the extent of rapes and sexual violence on university and college campuses? How about workplace violence that can also lead to abductions and sex crimes?

129

Crucial advice: Children and teenagers of course do not like to *check in*, so make it a firm rule. You are the parent and you are in charge. Start a strict policy of checking in with one another.

Can't afford a cell phone? Yes you can. Purchase a cheap phone and plan, or buy a "disposable phone," also known as a prepaid phone or TracPhone. They are inexpensive and you can buy minutes (airtime) as you need them. No expensive plans. You can buy a prepaid phone kit from most any cell phone carrier, department store, or major pharmacy.

The cost of a kit, including charger, is anywhere from $10 to $30 and the phone can include text messaging. The minute cards (airtime) are as low as $15. A start-up cost of $10 to $20 is a really good deal when it comes to saving a life. Buy $10 or $15 worth of airtime each month and restrict usage to emergencies and calls home. Only $10 a month to protect your child.

If your children, including teenagers, are going to someone's home, have them call you on your house phone or your cellular phone from that home phone. This will leave a caller ID number. It only takes a few minutes.

If your teenager is going out on a date or to have fun for the day, "par-tee," have them call as soon as they arrive and have them leave a location. You also need to know who they are with. If they do not call you, then you call *them*. Make this a rule.

Parents, I know this will be really, really hard, but try to just say thank you for calling. No Twenty-One Questions. Don't make these check-in calls discussions or arguments. Make them very brief loving experiences. Not "finger gepoken" experiences.

These check-in calls may also discourage would-be assailants. When they realize you are notifying others of your whereabouts, they are less likely to attack. There are simply too many witnesses and too much information.

Like I said earlier, snap a picture of the person you meet and make light of the picture. Then text it to someone. Just last month, a young, attractive female soldier from Ft. Bragg, N.C. was at a bar, and disappeared after leaving with a male employee of the bar. This was a capable girl and she was supposedly with someone she knew. She supposedly sent a text message to someone saying she was home. Did she send that text? What happened? She has now vanished; pray she will be found okay. Remember, "hard target."

Predators are usually secretive. Talkative and engaging perhaps, but guarded. That will become apparent when you start asking personal questions. They will usually try to avoid your questions, provide very little information, or become nervous. However, keep in mind some of them are great liars and actors. They can build up this huge false persona. This is why Internet stalkers are so dangerous. On the Internet your sense of understanding and reality are diminished. A forty-year-old pervert suddenly becomes a twenty-year-old hunk. Once you meet up with him, he will strike like a snake.

Want to know one good way to determine if someone is *nervous* or *stressed out*? Watch the carotid arteries on both sides of their neck. When someone is nervous or anxious, the arteries will usually be more pronounced and pulsating. Watch these arteries when the person is relaxed compared to when they are stressed or hyper. Look at their skin tone. It may become pale or flushed. Eye contact is important. People have a hard time looking you in the eye when they are being deceptive or lying. Of course they could just be shy.

Hopefully, every child and teenager has a curfew. It doesn't matter if they are twelve or nineteen years old. As long as they live in your house they need to follow your rules and obey a curfew. Teenagers can drive a parent crazy with complaining and arguments. Don't argue with them; just make it a rule. If they break those rules then make them explain what they did wrong. During the discussion, be firm and maintain control of the conversation.

Teach your children that there are consequences for not obeying your rules. This is the first step whereby children later learn to obey rules and laws outside their home. After a calm two-way discussion, you must give your children some form of punishment. I used to make my children write a paper telling me what they did wrong and why it was wrong. They knew the paper had to be written properly, or they would have to go back and do it over. Many years later, after they had grown up and left home, they told my wife and me they hated that punishment, but learned a lot by having to think and write about their mistakes. Sometimes this works better than restricting them to their room or house for the next ten years. Punishments need not be harsh and lengthy, just consistent.

Did you know that in America over **six hundred thousand young girls and women** are raped every year? That is over one rape every minute of the day. Women between the ages of sixteen and twenty-four years are at the highest risk. Most young women are raped by someone they know, not a stranger. For college students, drugs and alcohol are often the culprits. Thousands of boys and young men are raped as well. Remember the figures you read in the earlier chapter?

Do you know where your child spends his or her time during the day or evening? Whom do they hang out with? Do you know what they are doing on the Internet? Are they surfing pornography or chatting with predators? Are they playing violent or sexual computer games?

You may want to place the computer in a location where it can be easily observed. You can also restrict violent and sexual contents on computers by using security settings and passwords. Most televisions and cable TV have parental controls as well. Use them!

You can buy **computer software that will allow you to play back computer activities** by each key stroke and screen shot. See what they are typing and what they are looking at every second. Invasion of privacy? Nonsense! These are your children—whatever their age. Protect them! Love them by

CHAPTER 6: PERSONAL AWARENESS AND PREVENTION

being a responsible and concerned parent. This also includes guardians. You are the parent.

Take time to sit down and talk to your children or foster children. And listen to them as well. Kids and teenagers are pretty smart. Make rules and follow up with consequences. That's how children learn and become good adults.

For those parents and so-called experts who want to argue that *strong* **violent and sexual video games** do not lead to poor judgment and acting out—wrong! It is a proven fact. Both teenagers and adults have committed rape and murder because of their obsession with these games and other so-called entertainment. Come on! No one can seriously believe that allowing children and teenagers to watch or play anything with extreme violent and sexual content is good for them. Everything in moderation.

Of course, violent and sexual media is not the only problem. A lack of good parental supervision and hanging out with the wrong person or group are two other factors. Want to argue this point? Why? If there is a slight chance this is true, then just say "NO!" to video games and movies with heavy-duty violence and sexual content. Just say "NO" to children and teenagers running around unsupervised.

How much do you know about *child pornography, family molestation, pedophiles, sexual predators, parental kidnapping, domestic and international slavery, date rape, etc.?* Learn more by researching the Internet (information and videos) or reading books. Talk to counselors at school and church.

Learn where **sexual predators and pedophiles are living in your area**. There are links provided at the end of this book. Is there a sexual offender living in your neighborhood? Visiting your home? Is your child or teenager going to his/her home?

There are national and state **sex offender registries** on the Internet that show you who committed sexual crimes and where they are living. The registry usually includes a picture, name, and address. Once you have identified a sexual predator living nearby, Google their full address. Google their name along with the crime they committed. The news articles you find may just scare you. With Google Earth and street-map view you may able to look at their home. Oh yeah, keep in mind they can do the same to you and your family members.

You may want to hire a **private investigator** to learn more about suspicious persons or places. Police have their limitations and restrictions. Don't play detective yourself and get hurt. You need to be careful and remain anonymous. A private investigator is in the information business. Let them discreetly collect information for you and take the risks. Let the PI help you assess the situation.

The second key to survival is *prevention*. This means being *prepared*. A number of programs and technology have been developed to assist law enforcement, department stores, and certain other businesses with locating missing children and adults as quickly as possible. Learn what these programs and technology encompass.

Find out if your schools, day-care facilities, and businesses you frequent use these programs and if they have *contingency plans* for missing-person reports. If a child or adult turns up missing, notify the appropriate supervisors and managers immediately and then notify the police. Most businesses now have a security program called **Code Adam**. It involves step-by-step procedures the managers and private security personnel must follow.

After you have contacted the authorities (LE and security), your next step is to call the national help organizations mentioned above and listed at the end of this book. Start a journal and write down the name and telephone number of every person you speak with. This includes the police, security personnel, schools, businesses, friends and associates, organizations, everyone. If you feel it is necessary, call the local FBI office or DHS-HSI. Just keep a journal of everyone you call and everything discussed. Always

CHAPTER 6: PERSONAL AWARENESS AND PREVENTION

obtain names, twenty-four-hour telephone numbers, case numbers, and other details.

Let's start looking at security devices and equipment. There are numerous commercial products available at a small cost. These products range from simple laminated **identification cards** to **Ground Positioning System (GPS)** tracking devices that work with your cellular telephone and computer. There are do-it-yourself **dental impressions** and **deoxyribonucleic acid (DNA)** kits. There are also educational **video tapes and books** for children—and much more. The educational tapes are excellent, but review them first so you can discuss the content with your child or teenager.

You can also buy **hidden (disguised) cameras** (sometimes called nanny or baby-sitter cameras) that will allow you to monitor sitters, house cleaners, and others in your home or office. There are **two-way radio monitors** that allow you to hear what is happening in another room or even in multiple rooms. You can buy **computer software** that allows you to monitor your child's activities on the Internet. Again, you can actually review everything your child or teenager does on the computer, key stroke by key stroke and screen shot by screen shot.

There was a horrible incident in which an intruder broke into a home, went upstairs, and savagely beat and raped a young teenager. Her parents never heard a sound until the poor girl managed to crawl downstairs to their room and wake them up. We have also heard of cases where intruders have snuck into houses and kidnapped children. Remember the Elizabeth Smart case.

A **home alarm and monitoring system** will protect you when you are at home and away. If you cannot afford an alarm system, purchase several two-way room monitor/transmitter radios and place them strategically around the house to hear what is happening from your bedside radio (receiver).

There are also inexpensive **doorknob alarms**, or **door braces** that make it impossible to push or slide a door open. There are self-contained **window**

alarms that will alert you to breaking glass or the window being opened. You can even buy self-contained **motion sensors** and **security cameras**.

It no longer takes a security company to provide you with expensive services. However, they are still the experts, and having the live monitoring is well worth the money. At the end of the book you will find the names of a few companies who sell these home and business security items.

A lot of small vendors sell laminated photo identification (ID) cards for your children. These ID cards usually contain a photograph, some biographical information, and single, tiny fingerprints. I'm not so sure how this $15 to $25 plastic ID card is going to assist you if your child turns up missing. There is not enough information on these cards to be of help. The picture and fingerprints are of little use. However, you can learn how to make a really good emergency ID card almost for free. I'll show you in another chapter.

If you do purchase one of the ID cards, make sure the commercial vendor is not keeping personal information stored on their computer for their own nefarious use. What? That's right! Many of these vendors type in all this personal information and then have it saved to their laptops. What are they doing with that information afterwards? Scary!

Having said that, it is a good idea for children, teenagers, and adults to have a laminated picture identification card on their person in the event of an accident. This should be kept in a purse or wallet. You can even place a copy in the glove box of your car and in other vehicles. More important than biographical data, the card should contain emergency contact information and medical alerts. Not just one name and telephone number, but multiple names, telephone numbers, and e-mail addresses.

My daughter was involved in a serious traffic accident years ago. A witness retrieved her cell phone and was able to determine my telephone number and was kind enough to call. It might help to enter telephone numbers in

CHAPTER 6: PERSONAL AWARENESS AND PREVENTION

the directory with first and last names. You can then add a duplicate entry with the names "Mom," "Dad," "Husband," etc.

If you have a pass code (pin number) on your cell phone, a helpful bystander may not be able to access your phone directory. I encountered the very same situation, and I was unable to determine emergency contact information for a young girl who was having an asthma seizure after her bad accident. I went through her entire wallet and two glove boxes. Nothing! I even tried contacting her local bank and asked *them* to try and contact her parents. The bank wasn't very helpful.

If I can make two recommendations right now, they are to buy a **home alarm system** and to buy a **personal GPS tracking device** for your spouse, children, or loved ones. This includes children and elderly with mental issues that may cause them to wander away from home. Purchase a service plan for a company to monitor your home alarm, and buy a service plan so you can monitor the GPS on your cell phone and computer. How much will this cost? How much is your loved one worth?

To start with, **home alarm systems** have become very portable and no longer require complicated wiring. Most of the door and window contacts interact with the main panel box through radio frequencies. They come with simple remote FOBS (similar to your car) that make arming and disarming your system a simple push of a button. We no longer race for the control panel when we come inside. We take the FOB with us as we walk out the door, turn the system on, and turn it back off before walking inside.

Most systems also contain a *panic alarm*, a *secret alarm*, and various other *emergency buttons*. Obviously the panic alarm will create a very loud noise, which will hopefully scare off the intruder and alert the monitoring service. We use ours to make the dog go crazy. You can even have a panic button installed in your bedroom and other locations. Should you be attacked and forced to turn off the system, you can enter a secret code that will give the appearance you are disarming the unit, but you are actually secretly alerting the security monitoring service of a distress situation.

An added bonus is you can have the security alarm company add smoke detectors that will be monitored by your service. One night, while I was out of town, my wife received a telephone call at 2:00 a.m. The security company told her the alarm battery was getting ready to die and they were alerting her that she would hear the system beep, and that she should not be alarmed (no pun intended). The alarm company came out to the house the next day and changed all the batteries in the smoke detectors and contacts for the doors and windows. The cost was something like $25.

It was suggested earlier that if a stranger comes to the door, take your telephone with you. If you have an alarm system with a FOB, you can also keep that in your hand.

These home alarm systems cost anywhere from $250 to $500 to install, and the monitoring service is around $35 to $45 a month. With these systems come warning display signs for your lawn (front and back) and stickers for your doors and windows. Use them. This alone will scare off most potential intruders. Congratulations! You have now become a hard target. That alarm system and warnings will probably be your number-one protection system, followed by the GPS devices.

Closed-circuit television cameras (**CCTV**) now come in self-install packages for anywhere between $100 and $500 depending on the number and type of cameras. Most of the cameras can operate at nighttime in very low light. Like home alarms, the units can be wireless and can be monitored over a laptop or computer from remote locations. They can even be monitored over your cell phone. You can program the system to start recording if a camera senses motion. Incredible! What effect will this have on anyone approaching your house or inside your place of business when they see these cameras strategically placed? If you cannot afford a CCTV system, you can buy fake cameras with little working red lights.

CHAPTER 6: PERSONAL AWARENESS AND PREVENTION

Install these at your front and back door. Congratulations again! You have become an even harder target.

If you do not have a **car alarm system** and a remote key FOB with a **panic button**, you can buy a system and have it installed in your car. Or, you can simply install a panic alarm system that comes with a FOB. It is programmed to sound your car horn, and you can even install a louder horn. It should also be programmed to make your headlights flash on and off.

When you are going to and from your car, in a parking lot or at home, carry this remote control FOB in your hand, day or night. Not only do panic buttons cause the car horn to sound, but they cause the headlights to flash so that your location can been seen in the dark. Obviously, if you think someone is watching or approaching you, activate the panic button.

When it comes to our children, we will spend $50 to $100 on school pictures or $75 to $150 for a yearbook. Every year we spend thousands of dollars on their clothes and sports. We will spend thousands more on their jewelry, parties, and field trips. But, how much will we spend to save their lives? We spend much more on ourselves and our spouses or partners. But how much will we spend to protect ourselves and our loved ones? You decide.

Imagine how fast your child or loved one can be located with a **personal GPS tracking device** that costs between $200 and $250 to purchase and between $30 and $40 a month for a service plan to monitor the device. A GPS tracking device can be placed on the body, or in a backpack, purse, or car. They come disguised as watches and bracelets. You can monitor the GPS device and easily determine your loved one's location and direction of travel from your cell phone, laptop, or desktop computer. When combined with a street map application, you can determine the house number where they are located. Go to Google Earth and Google street-map view and look at an actual picture of the house, building, or field.

A personal GPS device can even be programmed to alert you when your child has wandered beyond a preset distance from your cell phone or computer. Set the distance for twenty-five or fifty feet, and as soon as they have moved past that point, the alarm will notify you. That's great for when your children are with you in a department store. There is another less expensive version that does nothing more than alert you when they move a certain distance from you.

A GPS device can determine how fast the device is traveling as well. If your child is supposed to be in school and they are traveling sixty-five mph, something is wrong. I wouldn't be surprised if the devices can soon be programmed to alert you when they exceed a certain speed. Set the alarm for ten mph, and you'll know if they are no longer walking.

What is this amazing device? A GPS is a cellular tower or satellite-based system that can triangulate (measuring angles to three known points) and locate the device on a continuous basis. By looking at the signal on a map display, you can see exactly where the device or person is located. You can watch them as they move and change locations by street and address. It is similar to the land navigation systems used in your car.

The GPS system is also used to locate a cellular telephone by triangulating off cellular towers or by using an internal GPS. If your loved one has a cellular telephone, let the LEO know immediately. They can get an emergency subpoena and the cellular service provider (carrier) will locate the phone. Make sure the phone is fully charged before leaving the house and tell your child or loved one to keep it turned *on*. Yes, they can be tracked when it is turned off in some cases, but know it is better to keep the cell phone turned on.

You have learned a little about my exclusive Individual Protection Packet (IPP). Many security companies sell USB flash (thumb) drives, bracelets, and other **electronic storage devices** that will allow you to record some of the same information listed in the IPP and Biographical Form, but much less information and for a lot more money. A little bit of information

CHAPTER 6: PERSONAL AWARENESS AND PREVENTION

is not enough to quickly locate someone or to conduct a successful investigation.

The IPP and Biographical Form were prepared by a very experienced investigator—ME! When completing the form, answer every question to its fullest and keep it updated. Include as much detail as possible in the form. When you hand the police officer or detective your thumb drive with all this information, ask the detective to go over it with you on the spot and to point out anything that may have been left out. This will not only benefit the police officer or detective on the scene, it will make a lasting impression in their minds. It will make the case personal.

For now, prepare the entire IPP for yourself, your children, and any other loved one. Keep all the original information and records in a secure and safe (dry) location. Never give out detailed personal information to others unless it is absolutely necessary. Always think **identity theft**, a whole new problem that is growing by leaps and bounds.

Regarding identity theft, you never want to provide someone with enough information to assume your identity for financial fraud or other crimes. This typically includes your full name, date of birth, and/or social security number. Criminals will often look for more details, such as your address and place of birth, but the first three items of information are enough to ruin your life.

Keep in mind that when you receive telephone calls and e-mails asking for your personal information, it may be a **scam or con**. Why would a bank or company ask you for your personal account information when they already have it on file? Tell them that! I bet you are going to get a great answer.

When someone calls you for information or money, ask them for their first and last name, the full name of their business, where they are located (complete address), their *main* number and their direct line or extension. Tell them to call back in fifteen minutes or call them back later. Google the phone number, business name, and address separately. Call information and get their telephone number and address. Call them back and see how the main number is answered. If they don't like that idea—tough.

Destroy trash that contains personal and sensitive information. Don't just throw it in the trash can. Don't put your personal information on **Facebook** and **MySpace**. **Social networking** can be dangerous—very dangerous. Teenagers are notorious for revealing personal information and posting compromising photographs online. You can block your profile and someone may still be able to gain access to your profile or page.

Facebook has removed over 2,800 known sex offenders from their website and MySpace has removed over 10,700 identified sex offenders. How many have gone undetected? Can you now understand the extent these predators will go to in order to find a victim?

Okay, here is how to check out a telephone number. Go to **www.addresses.com** and **www.whowhere.com**. You can also try typing the number directly into the Google search box. Enter the telephone number and start searching. Then enter the business name and search. Last, enter the address and search. Do all of this step by step as opposed to entering all the information at once. These search engines have what is known as a reverse lookup. If they can't find their telephone number, they can possibly find it through their business name or address.

You can even use Skype to identify telephone numbers and people. Search by number, name, e-mail address, etc. Don't know what Skype is? It is a free telephone service over your computer. We use it to call our boys overseas—for free. You can also use your computer cam.

Want to know who is on your telephone **caller ID** or a **scrap piece of paper you may find**? Search it on the above websites. Try yourself as an experiment. Private investigators can help if you are unsuccessful or want more information on a person, place, or thing. A PI can run a telephone-number search and a person's name for $25 to $50 and obtain a lot of information. We are talking ten to twenty pages for a comprehensive report.

Once you have completed the IPP, transfer or scan what you can onto a **USB flash drive**, also known as a jump drive or **thumb drive**. These devices are also called **portable electronic storage devices** and can hold anywhere from 1 gigabyte (GB) to 8 GB of data or information. A thumb drive is about the size of a thumb. But compact versions can be found in much smaller sizes.

Some USB thumb drives come with a key-ring attachment. Perfect! You may not want to carry the thumb drive on your key ring, but it makes it easier to find and you can securely attach it inside a purse, briefcase, or backpack. USB thumb drives can be purchased with both password protection and encryption (coded), so they are secure if lost or stolen.

How much space do you need? Think of an entire Individual Protection Packet as an individual's "file." Since each file will contain official records and images, they will use a lot of space. If you have only two to four files to place on your thumb drive, then 1 to 2 GB should be large enough. So, one thumb drive can be used for several family members. Just treat it like your wallet or purse. Hang onto it and guard it closely. Be careful; a 4 GB high-end *encrypted* thumb drive can cost as much as $50 and is often used by bankers and executives. You may want a less sophisticated version that is *password* protected and costs half that amount. I always think *secure*. Why risk identity theft and personal protection to save a few dollars?

Carry the thumb drive with you in the event of an emergency, especially when traveling. Keep a copy at work or give a copy to another close family member. Give a copy to a trusted neighbor. Label the thumb drive with your name and telephone number in the event it is lost.

Crucial advice: Keep the information and files updated on your home computer and your portable USB thumb drive. If you do not have a computer and scanner at home, find someone to help you put this information together. No excuses!

What about **medical and dental records**? Yes, you can get your personal physician to give you an electronic/digital copy to download on your USB thumb drive. Your dentist can also provide an electronic copy of your dental X-rays to download on your thumb drive. This includes individual X-rays of your teeth and a full panorex (panographic) X-ray of your entire mouth. Or, just keep a "hard" (nondigital) copy of the records at home. Yes, keeping a copy of the hard records at home is fine as long as you can get access to them immediately. This may not be the case if you are on a trip.

You will have to keep your **dental impression** and **DNA samples** in a safe secure place at home as well. You can submit the DNA sample for profiling and/or full genome sequencing (FGS). You can request that this genetic fingerprinting remain confidential or you can have it added to a national DNA database. Once you have the written results of the DNA sample, include them on your thumb drive.

You also need to produce and save a short **video clip** of your loved one speaking and moving before a camcorder or smartphone. The video should be no longer than fifteen seconds. This video clip also produces a **voice print**. Both the video clip and the voice print will be useful to LEOs and federal agents.

The video clip can also be used by the media to broadcast to the public and will of course have more of an impact than a simple photograph. It allows the audience to see your entire body and build, as well as your face. They can hear your voice and identify your accent or colloquialism. More important, it is a personal plea for help. Which would you better remember on television, a photograph or the short video clip of a person speaking to you and asking you for your help? However, make sure you have both a video clip and still photographs.

Yes, voice prints can be measured by instruments and used for formal identification. There is even the capability of **facial recognition** by computer. Some may dispute this technology, but it exists and is still being perfected. If anything, this voice recording can be used to compare with future voice recordings. LEO will find it very useful for interviewing witnesses. They will be able to play the video for, say, a hotel attendant or waitress.

How do you make this video clip? Start with a close-up of your loved one's face and then zoom out for a full body shot as they are introducing themselves. At the end zoom in on the face once more for a big smile. For example, "Hi, my name is Jane Smith and I am sixteen years old. I live in Los Angeles, California. If you are watching this video clip, then I might need your help. Thank you (with a smile)." If you are using a smartphone without zoom capability, start with the person's face and then walk backwards until you have the full body in your screen. Then walk forward again. You will want to rehearse at first and then take several clips to pick a favorite. Make sure your loved one moves around in the video clip using facial and hand expressions.

Use a light-colored, simple background that will not distract from the subject. Make sure there are not any background noises to interfere with a voice print. This is not a glamour shot or a movie. Your loved ones should dress normally—like they would any other day. If their hair is tied back, then they can let it loose while talking. They can even remove their glasses at the end of the video clip.

Again, try to keep the video clip to fifteen seconds. This is a video clip you can share with friends and searchers. It can be used by the media. The point of the fifteen seconds is to make it quick and to minimize the storage capacity. You can always make an extra thirty-second clip for use by investigators. In that longer video, have the person make a full 360-degree *slow* turn. Keep them talking. Remember to let the hair down and take the glasses off during the video recording. You can also zoom in on any distinguishing features, such as a scar or tattoo. Okay, so that's two video clips: one for fifteen seconds and another for thirty seconds.

It is suggested that you keep a copy of this short video clip on your cell phone, along with the photographs I will suggest later. **There is nothing faster and more powerful than sending out multiple text messages and emails with photographs.** I would suggest sending out a separate text message with the staged video clip to avoid downloading problems.

Here is something else I am going to suggest. If you are involved in a child custody case, or if you have an estranged spouse or someone else you fear, keep a few photographs of them on your cell phone and computer. The police might just need those photos ASAP. You may also want to know where they live and the vehicle(s) they drive. Where do they work. If need be, hire an attorney and private investigator for legal protection and to find answers. If a child turns up missing in a child custody case, the police will needs clues to act upon as quickly as possible. Does your situation involve an angry ex-spouse or boyfriend/girlfriend? The same advice applies.

Someone asked me if they could do this for their pet. Sure, just think about what you need to record and save it to a thumb drive. When I asked him about his wife, he just laughed. Okay!

Chapter 7

THE INTERNET

Through this book you will learn how to protect yourself and your family from *violent* and *sexual* content and encounters over the Internet, also known as the World Wide Web (www) or just the web. There is so much to learn and know about *Internet security* I could devote an entire book to this one topic. Instead, I am going to provide some information and then suggest you go to other websites to learn more.

I am also going to suggest you read a lengthy article written by Michael Nuccitelli, titled **"iPredator."** It can be purchased from Amazon.com and it is an incredible and detailed article about various threats one faces over the Internet. Mr. Nuccitelli is the owner of iPredator, Inc. and has a fantastic website. Go to www.darkpsychology.co. That's not a mistake; there is no letter *m* at the end. (If you use an *m* you will be directed to a rather strange-looking site.) The point is, his article will give you very valuable advice. Visit his website and read about *cyber bullying*. Children have actually committed suicide as the result of cyber bullying.

Did you know there are predators who go online and try to convince people to commit suicide? One man was actually convicted of this crime. Do you remember the recent case in which several young girls (cyber bullies) caused another young girl to commit suicide? They may be charged as well.

The FBI Internet Crime Complaint Center (IC3) has very good information on Internet threats and a section devoted to *cybercrimes*, as does the DHS, ICE, and Cyber Crimes Center (C3). I provided links to these agencies in the back of the book. You can contact them to report crimes as well.

In addition to learning about the personal threats over the Internet, you are about to get some free advice on cybercrimes. Cybercrimes are a growing threat, and involve *computer hacking, identity theft, stalking*, and *pornography*. Pornography includes *child pornography* and stalking includes both Internet stalking and physical stalking. There are ways to protect yourself and your loved ones from sophisticated *Internet predators*. Is the Internet bad? No! You just need to be aware of the threats over the Internet and avoid temptations. Parents! Your children need you to help them avoid these temptations.

Social networks such as Facebook, My Space, and online dating services can be hunting grounds for these violent offenders and sexual predators. Even Craigslist became an instrument for sex and predators. Predators use these social networks, chat rooms, and blogs to lure you in, and once you are hooked, with the little information you reveal, they can come find you— wherever you are. Learn how to protect personal information over the Internet and on the telephone. Learn how to avoid traps and getting hooked.

Remember what was said in the previous chapter about social networks. Don't advertise your personal information on Facebook, MySpace, and online dating services. Social networking can be dangerous— very dangerous. Teenagers and some adults are notorious for revealing personal information and posting compromising photographs online. You can block your profile, but someone with a little experience will still be able to gain access to your profile page.

What is your personal information? It includes your full legal name, complete address where you live, telephone numbers, e-mail addresses, date of birth (DOB), place of birth (POB), social security number (SSN), and any other biographical data. Why openly advertise any of this information? If someone wants it, let them ask you. Then decide what personal information you want to provide.

I am stressing this point. Give me certain parts of this personal information, and I can find the missing pieces of the puzzle to put your life together. Once I have what I need, I can come find you anywhere. I can steal your identity and take all of your money over the Internet. I can even open more credit accounts and spend money using your name. It creates a security and financial nightmare.

Facebook has removed over 2,800 known sex offenders from their website and MySpace has removed over 10,700 identified sex offenders. After some resistance, Craigslist agreed to remove undesirable content, which include contact information for sexual encounters and prostitution. How many predators have gone undetected?

Can you now understand the extent these predators will go to in order to find a victim? Why would these companies even argue about these matters? Probably because of money and the so-called argument of individual rights. Very sad, but that is the state of our society and world today—do whatever you want even though others will be seriously harmed.

Parents *must* wake up and realize the Internet can be both a danger and a temptation to your child. You must understand the threats and temptations and monitor your children and teenagers' activities over the Internet. They are playing with a deadly time bomb and you can prevent their harm by taking certain precautions, which include setting certain restrictions and rules. That's what parents do—set rules and teach children to obey rules. Even adults need to be aware of this Internet threat and exercise extreme caution.

Always practice computer and Internet security for protection against computer hackers and cybercrimes. Hopefully, you are using a good Internet firewall and virus protection and keeping them updated. Learn about *phishing* (pronounced fishing), *e-mail frauds, computer hackers,* etc. Learn more about *spyware* (collection software), *malware* (malicious software), and *keystroke logging* (duplication software).

You can visit the following government websites to learn more: http://www.fbi.gov/scams-safety/ and http://www.usa.gov/Citizen/Topics/Internet_Fraud.shtml. Or, just Google each word or term.

Spyware and malware are secret software programs downloaded on your computer while you surf the Internet. Keystroke logging is also secretly downloaded and will duplicate your keystrokes to steal your information and activities. This malicious software can be hidden in e-mails that, once opened, dig their way into your computer system and hide. They are little cyber monsters.

Bottom line: Always use a good Internet firewall and virus protection. Learn more about viruses and spyware. The best protection is *encryption.* You can purchase and use encryption software for your computer, documents, and emails.

Personally, I use **Trend Micro**. Read about their Titanium Security software. The good thing about ordering over the Internet and downloading the program is you can buy a package deal that will allow you to protect up to three computers. When you change computers you can call a Micro Trend technician and transfer those programs to new or other computers. They will also provide you with valuable assistance over the Internet or by phone.

Crucial advice. If you do not recognize an e-mail address, do not open that e-mail. Delete the e-mail and then delete it from your computer's trash can.

Here is another free tip. On your Internet screen go to "tools," usually on the top right corner. Click on tools and then select "internet options," usually towards the bottom of the list. Delete all choices: browsing history, temporary files, cookies, saved passwords and web form information.

You should take this step every time you exit the Internet. There is an "automatic delete" box to select. You can check the block that reads "delete history." But I suggest deleting everything by checking each block. It only takes a minute. There are other features in "internet options."

Here is another tip: never open hyperlinks from an e-mail. Copy the link and then paste it directly into the URL address block. Try adding an *s* to the end of the http://, e.g., https://. The *s* will take you to a secure link if one exists for that website. It usually does. If the site is secure, you will also see a closed padlock to the right indicating you are on a secure website. Sometimes the padlock is at the end of the URL search block or at the bottom of the page. The small padlock icon may be gold in color.

One last tip: always use strong passwords along with your Internet protection software to protect against hackers. Each password should contain uppercase and lowercase letters along with numbers and special characters. These passwords need to be changed from time to time. Just write down the passwords on a paper in the event you forget them. Do not store these passwords in a document on your computer. Just keep the paper hidden nearby for easy access. Don't leave it out in the open for anyone to see or take.

These tips are especially important for conducting financial transactions over the Internet, to include banking and commercial accounting for paying bills and purchasing merchandise.

Take the time to learn more about Internet security! Research the NCMEC website and the FBI website to learn more about child pornography and Internet safety. While you are on NCMEC, visit their learning tool for children, NetSmartz. Get your children started right away.

You may want to set "parental restrictions" on your computer and set the security features to at least medium-high, if not high. This will restrict offensive and violent websites, pictures, and graphics. Just go back to "tools," "internet options," and click on the tab that says, "security."

Another option is to place the computer in an open area where you can monitor your children and teenagers' activities. If the computer is in a room, make it a rule that they must leave the door fully open for your spontaneous checks.

You can also purchase software programs that will record all activities on your computer, key stroke by key stroke. You can even determine how long a user stays on any given screen shot.

Chapter 8

PHYSICAL SECURITY

This is a quick chapter to familiarize you with the term and concept of *physical security*. You have already read some material on this subject. Physical security pertains to protecting homes, buildings, and other facilities or structures, both outside and inside.

Physical security can also pertain to *information technology* (IT) as it relates to computer systems and electronic storage. There are private investigators and security companies that specialize in this field.

The intent of physical security is to *prevent* an intrusion. This is the same thing we want when it comes to personal security: to prevent an attack from happening in the first place. Another way to think of physical security is to *deter* and *delay* intrusions (attacks), since it is almost impossible to stop a determined and sophisticated criminal.

The goal is to intimidate the intruder and scare him away. This will happen if your security appears to be tight, meaning you are a hard target. If the criminal is actually breaking in (attacking), the second goal is to delay him and notify the police before any harm is done or something valuable is stolen.

Okay, we have prevent, deter, and delay intrusions and attacks. Terminology is always good to know when speaking with professionals. It reminds me of that old joke, "Top ten reasons why I did not make it in the CIA: I thought Cloak and Dagger was a rock group."

Physical security includes the locks on your doors and windows. But locks are not enough, and cheap inexpensive locks are worthless. Let's just look at a small list of physical-security protections used at homes (and businesses). I will list them in the order of outside to inside your house. *Boo!* Of course you will need to decide what equipment and services you want to purchase.

- Security guards, canine patrols, and bodyguards.
- Barriers such as walls, fences, and gates. This can include natural barriers such as thorny hedges, and it can include security bars on the outside that cover your doors and windows. These are very popular in high-crime areas.
- Warning signs and stickers on the property grounds, doors, and windows.
- Indoor and outdoor lights such as street lights, porch lights, and floodlights. Lights are very important and inexpensive.
- Curtains, blinds, and other window coverings.
- Locks, deadbolts, chain locks, and locking bars for both your doors and windows. I mean real locks, not the cheap locks used during typical home construction.
- Closed-Circuit Television cameras (CCTV) for the outside and inside. Real or fake.
- Alarm systems that protect your doors, windows, and garage, to include motion detectors and a monitoring service. Make sure to get a least two remote FOBs, if not three.

- Camera and radio devices that allow you to see and hear what is happening in other rooms.
- Weapons such as handguns, shotguns, rifles, stun guns (Tasers), and mace.
- Safe for your weapons and your valuables.
- The right dog is an excellent preventative measure, especially a trained dog.

Home or business alarm system: You have already read about some of these security measures. As mentioned earlier, if you want a good suggestion, purchase an alarm system for your home, along with a monitoring service. This should be a priority on your checklist. This will include posting the alarm warning signs around your house and placing warning stickers on your doors and windows.

These alarm systems can include a remote FOB to activate your alarm system from outside your house or from any room inside the house. The system can include a panic button, either remote FOB or individual panic buttons can be installed in the bedroom and around your house. You can also install smoke detectors that will alert the monitoring service.

The cost for this security feature is an initial start-up of $200 to $500 and a monthly cost of approximately $35 to $45 a month. What is life worth, if not the valuables inside your home or business?

Vehicle/car alarms: Most vehicles come with a remote-control key FOB to lock and unlock your doors and trunk. Another feature on that FOB is the *panic* button. Push that and the horn start starts blaring and the headlights and taillights start flashing. That provides excellent personal security for both day and night, and is so simple. When going to and from your vehicle, keep that FOB in your hand and your finger on the panic button. Do you remember what was said above regarding this feature?

If your car did not come with a remote FOB, you can have a system installed. You want a remote FOB with a long range. Even on new cars, some have a short distance and some have a longer distance. You want to be able to activate that panic alarm at the greatest distance possible for when you are in those really large parking lots.

As far as an actual car alarm, most newer cars come with a built-in alarm system, but if not, an alarm can be installed after purchase. I strongly recommend a car alarm system, but very highly recommend a panic alarm with a remote key FOB.

We also talked about **OnStar**. Again, I highly recommend OnStar in your vehicles for security and other reasons.

Closed-Circuit Television cameras (CCTV): These can be used outside and inside your house or your business. You can have them professionally installed or buy self-installation packages with two to six cameras. You can view these cameras from a television or monitor, or remotely through your computer, desk laptop, or cell phone. They can even be set up with a motion detector alarm. If you are away and the alarm goes off, take a look and see what is happening, no matter where you are. The cameras can record in very low-light environments using inexpensive infrared capabilities (IR), or they can have nighttime capabilities. True nighttime cameras are more expensive. Another thing to consider is the resolution. You want high resolution so that when you zoom in on a face, the picture does not become distorted. These recordings are usually digital and make great evidence for you, the police, and prosecutors. They are stored on the system's internal hard drive and can be directed to computer files to access later.

The start-up cost for a *self-installed* CCTV system is between $200 and $500. It usually depends on how many cameras come with the kit. Installation can include hard wires or electronic remote connections between the cameras and the main system, which resembles a typical cable TV/DVR box. Setting up the system to include the remote viewing can be a little tricky. You may want to hire someone for the installation. This will cost a few hundred extra for labor.

If you cannot afford a CCTV, an alternative is to install a few fake cameras at the front and back doors. They have a small red light that blinks, making someone think they are real. Guess that's better than nothing.

Outside lights: It is also suggested that you utilize lights around the outside of your home. Most homes already have porch and patio lights, as well as lights for the garage doors. Installing floodlights on the corners of your roof is relatively inexpensive, as are the light bulbs and electricity.

Today's light bulbs are low wattage (less power) and can be left on all night, every night, over a period of a year, maybe even two years, before needing to be replaced. Look into compact fluorescent lamps (**CFL**) and even better light-emitting diodes (**LED**). Again, look for lower watts (lower numbers) to save power. The brightness is measured by lumens. The higher the number, the brighter the light. You are not lighting up a stadium or your neighbor's bedroom window. You (and your neighbors) want just enough light to allow anyone to see through the darkness and into the shadows.

The typical outside floodlight is halogen, and most people use a 75- to 90-watt light. There are in fact "outside" flood lights made in CFL. The little twisty bulb is contained inside typical-looking floodlight housing. CFL floodlights last longer than halogen outdoor flood lights and are cheaper in the long run because of the lower wattage. Even with a Lowe's representative by my side, it took us a while to find the outdoor floodlight. I replaced my 90-watt halogen floodlights with a 23-watt CFL and got the same brightness.

If you do not want to be bothered with turning the lights on and off every day, or if you travel, you can use a timer, nighttime sensor, or motion detector—or any combination of these. If it only costs $50 to $100 to replace all the CFL lightbulbs once a year, then that is a good investment in your security and safety. It will add about $35 to $45 to your electric bill—per year. This is smart for when you are away from home. It is smart for when you come home at nighttime. About $10 to $20 a month for this important security measure. What is your life worth?

Locks and deadbolts: As far as your door lock and deadbolt, make sure both the door and the door *frame* are strong enough to withstand a powerful kick. If you use a door chain, that chain and the screws securing it to the door will also need to be strong enough to withstand a hard shove or a strong kick. These chains and hardware need to be strong. You may want to consider replacing your wooden doors and frames with metal, metal housing, or at least hardwood and larger screws. Softer woods commonly used in construction are not sufficient. One good kick or shoulder, and the wood and screws shatter.

You need to purchase and install quality door locks and deadbolts. This includes for your windows and other access points. It can get a little expensive, so you may want to do this in phases. In addition to the lock on your doorknob, you need to have a deadbolt. Listen, you want to keep your doors and windows locked, day and night. The really crazy predators will make a daytime entry and the home invaders will as well—because they want you to be inside. We often keep a key in the deadbolt on the inside. Instead of keeping the doorknob locked, and risk locking ourselves out of the house, we just twist the deadbolt.

I also recommend using **door and window bars (jams)** on the inside. Just prop them up against the door knob and place them in the inner frames of your sliding doors and windows. You can buy professionally made door and window jams, or you can make them yourself. If you like fresh air in the house, use a jam that will allow the window to open only an inch.

You can also buy the small, **portable, self-contained alarms** that hang from the doorknob or window. If someone shakes the device, it wakes up and screams at you. Sort of like a baby. Take them with you on a trip and use them in your hotel room. The small, portable alarm boxes cost anywhere from $30 to $50. You can attach them to other items, such as your purse or briefcase, car door, gun safe, lunch, etc.

Batteries: Let's talk about batteries for a second. Many of the devices I mention need batteries. I suggest you buy the *lithium* batteries. They supposedly last eight times (2x through 8x) longer than regular batteries. Energizer makes lithium batteries in all sizes, and they can be found at most all major department and hardware stores, as well as most major pharmacies. They usually come in a blue package with the letter *e* in a circle. You can use them in all your electronic devices to avoid frequent replacement. A four-pack of AA or AAA batteries costs about $8. When you consider how long they last, it is a better value. Use them in your alarm contacts, flashlights, cameras, room monitors, alarm clocks, computer mouse, etc.

Flashlights: Speaking of flashlights, please buy several small, portable flashlights and place them around your home and in your car. You want one by your bedside. Carry one with you in your purse or backpack. Again, look at the lumens to determine brightness. A good quality LED flashlight will cost between $30 and $50. When I say "quality," I mean that they are waterproof, will not easily break if dropped, and provide efficient lighting.

They even make **stun-gun flashlights**. If someone sees you with an ordinary flashlight, which actually works, they may get a bit of a shock when you stick it to them. These flashlights will cost about $70 to $80. They even come disguised as cell phones.

Chemsticks: I suggest having several plastic chemical lights (glow sticks or chemsticks) like we use in the Army and law enforcement. Snap one, shake, and toss it where you need light. They will last anywhere from a few hours to twelve hours. If you have a power outage they are very useful. Did your vehicle break down? Place one on the roof of your car and throw one about one hundred feet (thirty yards) behind your vehicle. Going running at night or trick-or-treating with your kids? Strap a mini chemstick on one of your arms.

Window coverings: Blinds and curtains are also important, so that intruders cannot see activities and valuable objects within your home.

This includes not leaving valuables on counters and tabletops in plain sight. If a thief can see your purse, wallet, cell phone, laptop, and other valuable items through the windows, they will attempt a smash and grab. This was also mentioned in regard to leaving valuables exposed in your car.

At nighttime, someone looking inside your home from the dark outside cannot be seen. But they can see you very well. They can also be looking in from a distance using binoculars, telescopes, or long-range zoom cameras. The same can be done in the daytime.

You can also buy window film/tint to put over your glass. This film comes in different thicknesses and shades of darkness. The biggest advantage to the security film is the strength. It is hard to penetrate and will protect the inside of your house from glass breakage by an intruder or a storm.

Fences and barriers: There is too much to be explained and discussed. If you decide you need natural barriers or man-made barriers (fences) around your property, talk to an expert and remember to get three estimates.

Room monitors: Most of us are familiar with the remote room monitors used with babies. These monitors, both audio and visual, can be used to enhance security or as an alternative device if you cannot afford a home alarm system. Remember the earlier story you read about the teenage girl who was savagely beaten and raped in her bedroom while her parents were asleep downstairs? Do you remember the story about the young girls having a sleepover when the predator walked right into the house and snatched one away, while the others watched? It is still hard to believe that no one taught any of these children to scream and yell when they were in danger. These small portable devices make a great security product.

I recently saw a new room monitor device that you could not only hear with, but you could view with over a small portable monitor or your cell phone. The system came with up to four small cameras. Another system included a camera that could be remotely controlled, and the camera could swivel side to side and up and down. They also come concealed in radios and clocks. The resolution is very good and they have a lengthy recording time. They can be activated by light, sound and motion. The cost? Just a few hundred dollars!

Motion detectors (portable): You can also buy small portable motion detectors for rooms and for outside. You can even install one on your mailbox or on a post to alert you when someone uses your driveway. Again, these battery-operated remote-controlled devices are inexpensive. Put one outside your door or on your patio. Put them in the rooms that are primary access points.

I recommend **Brick House Security** for most of your security needs. Look through their tabs on "Home & Family," "Business & Government," and "Police & Investigators." Check out their "How-to Guides" to learn about certain equipment and products. Their search bar works very well, but I find their sales representatives to be very helpful. I have actually had them suggest better items at lower prices than what I was asking about. They guarantee all of their products and have an excellent return policy.

You can contact a number of security companies for more advice as it pertains to your home. You can also learn a lot over the Internet. I personally use **ADT Security**. As mentioned above, they have provided us with excellent service over the years.

There is so much more to write on physical security and other security measures you can take at home, work, school, and other locations. This includes travel. Buy those portable alarm systems and take them with you. Hang them on the doorknobs and stick them to the windows. If your children are staying in another room, bring the audio/visual monitoring devices with you. At this point, you know enough to start your own research.

Chapter 9

YOUR EMERGENCY IDENTIFICATION CARD

Everyone needs to carry an *Emergency Identification Card* on their person. You can keep this card in your purse or wallet or just stick it in your back pocket. Keep a card in your car in the glove box and center console. You can put a card in your child's backpack or your backpack and briefcase. If you are at the beach or swimming, carry a card in your pocket or bag. If you are traveling, stick them in your luggage.

You may want to consider an emergency medical bracelet or necklace for major medical conditions. Do a little research on this topic. Research is all about *knowledge—awareness and prevention.*

One of the leading causes of death for emergency medical traumas is emergency medical errors due to the lack of vital medical information. There are others such as loss of blood. It would be nice if we could teach every person in America how to stop bleeding, treat shock, and perform cardiopulmonary resuscitation (CPR). How many people are aware that the procedures for CPR changed in 2010? You can also do a variation of CPR involving only chest compressions.

The information you provide on your *Emergency Identification Card* is sensitive and should be protected, but is vital to your emergency care. Remember, you may be unable to communicate. Most of this information is already listed on your driver's license and other identification cards, so don't let your concern for personal security override your need to provide vital information on the E-ID.

The Emergency Identification Card (E-ID) will assist with missing-person and emergency medical situations. Two for one. It will help identify you in the event you have an accident and you are unable to communicate. The card will identify your loved ones or other emergency contacts; and it will provide vital medical information Emergency Medical Services (EMS) personnel may need immediately on the scene or in a hospital.

This Emergency Identification Card can be easily made at home and laminated to protect it from water and destruction. Your personal E-ID can be computer generated, if you want it to look nice, or handwritten. Just use a heavy paper that can be purchased at most office supply stores. Even an index card can be cut down to size. Remember, you may want to make several cards to keep in different locations.

Another option is to go online and Google "emergency medical information." There are some websites that will allow you to enter all the information below and then print out their version of an E-ID. One site in particular allows you to print the card in different sizes.

However, it is recommended that your personal card contain a small photograph of your face. In the event you are unconscious, EMS can immediately determine the card is yours without having to compare it with other identification or investigate further. No sense in wasting valuable time.

Sheets (or pouches) of clear plastic laminate can be purchased. Some are self-adhesive (self-sealing) and some are heat sealed. Obviously, the heat-sealed laminate will require a small laminate heating machine. The heavy

CHAPTER 9: YOUR EMERGENCY IDENTIFICATION CARD

paper, laminate, and heat-sealing machine can be purchased at Staples, Office Depot, Office Supply, Office Max, etc. You may find everything you need at Target or Walmart. Go online.

If you want to use heat-sealed laminate sheets, but you do not want to purchase a heat machine, check with any of the office supply stores or even your local pharmacy to determine if they have a heat-sealing machine available for customer use.

You can even handprint this information and place it is a small sealable plastic bag to prevent damage. You can fold up a copy and stick it in your wallet.

However, if you do not have access to a computer, or do not know how to use a computer, you are encouraged to find a friend who will help you through the entire process of producing the E-ID and the Individual Protection Packet with the Biographical Form. You can consider hiring someone to help you put all this information and these items together. Perhaps a relative, trusted neighbor or someone from your church will help.

A typical driver's license or other identification card is 3 ¼ inches x 2 inches, if you want this E-ID to fit into a standard wallet. Remember, the laminate sheet (or pouch) will make the card a little larger, so you may want to reduce the size of the actual paper card.

You can use both sides of the E-ID, allowing for plenty of information. Put your contact information on one side and your medical information on the other side. Again, you should add a small photograph to the E-ID. Add the emergency medical symbol as well, or simply type *Emergency Medical Card* along the top on both sides in bold red. Do something to make the card stand out for EMS to find easily.

Include your full name on this card along with the names for all your emergency points of contact (POC). Not just one person, but two or three. When you include a POC's telephone numbers, please provide all of their numbers and identify the type, e.g., home=H, work=W, cellular=C pager=P, etc. You should also provide both a personal and a work e-mail address. The goal is to enable someone to reach your emergency POCs as *fast* as possible.

Remember the earlier example when I happened upon a serious traffic accident? The injured girl was having a severe asthma attack and could not speak. She was barely conscious and at first we thought she could be having a seizure. We could not find any POCs or anything about her medical condition in her purse or car. One of the passengers said her parents were on a trip to the beach. It took EMS and the police about fifteen minutes to respond, but it seemed like an hour.

Always call 911 first in the event of any emergency. Then call the POCs. If you do not get an answer, leave a *detailed* message with your name and *all* your contact telephone numbers. You should also send a text message and an e-mail.

Another thing to consider if you choose to keep your cell phone locked: you may be able to at least display a number on the main screen. Don't use your cell phone telephone number. Use a POC's cell phone number.

Here is some of the information you will want to consider for your E-ID. Remember, like your Individual Protection Packet, you want to keep information current and updated.

Your **blood type** is helpful. My daughter had to argue this point once with a physician assistant (PA). She asked the PA for a test to determine her blood type. The PA stated that hospitals can quickly identify your blood type and will do so before giving you blood. However, EMT personnel may need to know your blood type on the scene. If you are traveling or overseas in a foreign country, it may be useful as well. Go to your local physician or clinic, or donate blood to Red Cross or a hospital. Tell the

CHAPTER 9: YOUR EMERGENCY IDENTIFICATION CARD

physician or technician you *want* to know your blood type. Everyone should know their blood type.

Your emergency contacts will be those people whom you want contacted. They will usually include your parents, spouse, or other close relatives or friends.

If possible, list your **personal physician** or other primary care giver on your E-ID. Include their full name and *all* contact numbers. This should include the office number, cell phone (if they are willing to provide it to you), and their emergency telephone numbers for evenings and weekends when they are closed.

List any **medical conditions** you have; for example, seizures, asthma, diabetes, high blood pressure, heart condition, migraine headaches, skin rashes, etc. List them in order of importance. If you have a heart condition on the scene, EMS may not want to use an Emergency Automated External Defibrillator (AED), which determines your heart rhythm and administers an electrical shock. If you have a pacemaker, they may not.

List all the **medications** you take along with the dosage and frequency, e.g., Losartan Potassium, 100 mg, daily.

List all **allergies** for *medication* (penicillin, etc.); *food* (peanuts, etc.); *insect/other* (bee stings, etc.); and *environmental* (latex, etc.)

You may want to include your **religious preference**.

Here is the information one more time. Again, keep several cards on your person or nearby.

- "Emergency Medical Information" or medical emblem/logo at the top
- Small photograph (face only)
- Your full name

- Physical address where you live or where someone can be contacted by the police
- Date of birth, or at least your age
- POCs (Include their first and last name, all telephone numbers, and all e-mail addresses)
- Medical conditions and issues
- Medical prescriptions and drugs you take, and how often
- All allergies
- Religious preference if desired

Example for POCs (use at least two if not three):

John Smith, Husband. H# 202-987-6543. W# 202-123-4567, x-123. C# 703-876-5432. john.smith5@fairfax.gov or jschallenger@yahoo.com

Okay, let's move on to your Individual Protection Packets, followed by the Biographical Form. This was the main purpose of me writing this book. Then all the other stuff started flying out of my head. I thought to myself, "Wouldn't it be something if this book actually prevented pain and suffering or saved lives?"

Chapter 10

THE INDIVIDUAL PROTECTION PACKET

Here is what you need to collect and put together for your Individual Protection Packet (IPP). There are eight items on your checklist. The Biographical Form is in the next chapter. Remember, you want a complete IPP for each loved one, and you want to keep this information updated.

Most of this information and most official records can be scanned and downloaded on your computer, so you can later transfer it to a USB flash drive (thumb drive). You can use a DVD if you like, but I suggest the thumb drive. For those who do not know, a DVD disc holds a lot more information than a CD. If you use a DVD, use a RW disc, so you can add and write over information, i.e., DVD-RW.

Remember, it is best to purchase an encrypted thumb drive that is at least *password protected*. Purchase a thumb drive that can hold multiple IPP files (for each person), with plenty of data and images. You may want to purchase at least a 4 GB (gigabyte) capacity, if not more. Go ahead and get the 8 GB if you have a large family or more than four persons. The photographs and electronic records (medical and dental) will consume a lot of space, as will the photographs and video clips.

For now, produce the Biographical Forms with the embedded (copy and paste) photographs. This is your number-one priority. Then go down to your local police station or sheriff's office and get the fingerprints—your second priority. Add the medical and dental records later. You can simply call the office or stop by for a personal visit. I always find face-to-face meetings work better. Again, tell the receptionist or office manager you want a digital (or electronic) copy of your medical or dental file and ask them to e-mail those files. Save them to your computer and then download to your thumb drive.

If they cannot provide the records in this format, tell them you need a hard copy for your home records. Ask them to use a *high-quality* setting when printing the documents. Items that cannot be copied and scanned will need to be stored in a secure location and in a safe container to protect them from water and other damage. Keep them locked up somewhere safely at home where you will have twenty-four hour access to them.

I would suggest buying a decent-sized safe for you home, as suggested in the earlier chapter. Again, this is a method to store and protect other valuables, such as jewelry, documents, etc. It is also a safe place to store weapons, but keep in mind that fast access to those weapons will be diminished unless you buy a safe with a fingerprint scanner or a number pad. One day I burned my left index finger pretty bad. Guess what? I couldn't use the fingerprint scanner for almost three weeks. This was not due to blisters; I actually burned off my fingerprints, and as most of you know, they grow back.

I mentioned high-quality printing in the above paragraph. Here is a tip about your printer that some people are not aware of. When printing you can go to "printer properties" and change your ink settings to three levels. high, standard, and fast (or draft). The lowest setting (draft/fast) saves almost half the ink and the difference is barely noticeable. I only use the standard and high settings for resumes and graphics.

CHAPTER 10: THE INDIVIDUAL PROTECTION PACKET

I will provide a certain amount of technical information for a better understanding of what you are doing and what we hope to achieve. Knowledge is…right, power! Are you ready to help your local Crime Scene Investigator (CSI) technicians with their forensics?

Forensics is short for *forensic science*. It is the broad spectrum of sciences to answer questions of interest to a legal system in relation to a crime or a civil action. The Latin word for forensic means "of or before the forum." There are over thirty categories, or subdivisions, of forensics, such as criminal forensics, anthropology (skeletal remains), chemistry, dactyloscopy (fingerprints), interviews, trace evidence, pathology, psychiatry, psychology, and much, much more. Very interesting topic to research.

1. **Biographical Form**: (See the next chapter)

2. **Photographs**: Take various photographs and keep them updated. These photos will include four *facial* pictures and four *full-body* pictures. You guessed it—all four sides. You may not use all of them, but the police will want them for various reasons. We will also produce two short video clips.

Of course, digital photographs work best. Remember, no excuses. If you do not own a digital camera, buy an inexpensive model or borrow one. The cameras and videos on *smartphones* might work, but they do not usually have the high resolution the detectives and media will find useful. No shortcuts.

These are not glamour shots. They should be realistic depictions of how a person looks every day under normal conditions. These photographs will be used by you and the detectives for **posters, text messages, e-mails, interviews,** and the **media**. They will be used during the **search and rescue**.

Should you take the photos with or without their glasses; or with their hair up or down? How about that baseball cap that never comes off? Take both. Also take pictures of distinguishing features, e.g., scars, tattoos, birthmarks, etc.

Here is an example of why the police will need all these photographs and video clips. Let's say someone three states away reports seeing a girl who looked like your daughter (or wife) in a department store with an older male. The witness states he and his wife only saw her from the front for a few minutes and she seemed scared or nervous. However, two witnesses also saw her from the side when they walked out of the store to the parking lot. At the time she was wearing her hair down and glasses. Within a minute, the detectives can transfer the photographs and video clips to the other police department and the LEO there can show them to the witnesses. Will this be better than a simple photograph of a person's face? Absolutely!

After you have downloaded these photographs, you can *copy and paste* them to the Biographical Form and reduce them to the size of say 2 inches x 2 inches. Once the Biographical Form is opened, the pictures can be expanded (enlarged), and again, copied and pasted to other documents and forms as needed. The police and detectives will find this *extremely* useful. You will find this very useful. As long as someone has a digital copy of this Biographical Form, they can open and use these photographs as necessary.

We are going to electronically store these photographs and video clips in several locations for fast and easy access. This will include your thumb drive, smartphone, and e-mail. If you do not have a smartphone or some other means to store these photographs electronically, then carry actual photographs (hard copies) with you. Keep several wallet-sized photographs and write certain biographical information on the back of each picture. Carry two sets of the facial and body series. Hopefully, you will start carrying your USB thumb drive with IPP files on every family member. Again, this thumb drive should be *password* protected.

CHAPTER 10: THE INDIVIDUAL PROTECTION PACKET

Here is what you can write on the back of the photographs: full name, DOB, race/sex, height/weight and the date the picture was taken. You can have these available to give to the police or security.

It is highly suggested that you keep the photographs and video clips on your smartphone for immediate use. Again, these photographs and videos can be quickly sent to others in a text message. Send a text message to the police officer or security personnel with the pictures and videos attached. In the text, include the above information and include what they were wearing and any important details of the disappearance.

Kathy CARY disappeared on May 28, 2012 at 12:30 p.m. Kathy is 18 yoa, Hispanic, female, 5'1" and 140 lbs with long black hair. She was last seen at the Houston Mall in Evergreen, TX. Kathy was wearing dark blue jeans, pink T-shirt with the Nike logo on the front, and light brown leather boots. She was last seen with a white male, 20 yoa, tall and skinny, long black hair, wearing faded blue jeans and a white T-shirt with a logo on the back. Kathy has a small tattoo of a red heart on her left wrist. Please forward this text message with photos to all your friends. If you know anything please text me back and call me at (905) 123-4567 and (905) 890-7654. My e-mail is kathysmom123@yahoo.com."

Don't forget to include *all* your contact information: cell phone, home phone, e-mail, etc. If someone has information, make it easy for them to reach you.

You do not need to send all the photos and videos. I would suggest the front facial and full body pictures, along with the fifteen-second video clip.

Keep copies of these photographs and videos on your computer, laptop, e-notebook, e-tablet, etc. Hopefully, you use good *internet firewall and virus protection software* to help stop hackers.

Send yourself an e-mail with all the photographs and both videos that you can later retrieve from your e-mail account with a simple search. You can send these e-mails from your smartphone if you have set up e-mail access.

In the subject block of the e-mail, use your file name (person's first and last name), age, and the content, followed by the date they were taken. For each photograph, give it a file name and view.

Subject block: John HENRY, Age 15, photographs and video clip-11Jan2012

Photo name: Susan CARY, Age 9, front face (or right face)-27Mar2012

Video name: Mary JASON, Age 28, 15 sec video (and 30 sec video)-2Apr2012

Now you can go into your e-mail account, search for the e-mail, by typing in "John Henry Age 15," and then forward it to everyone who needs the photographs and video clip. You can also create an e-mail folder in your account titled; "All IPP." Put all your family members in that folder.

Why did I capitalize all letters in their last names? So the last name will never be confused as the first name. This is a technique LEOs will recognize.

Here is how to take the four *facial pictures*. Take a facial picture from the bottom of the neck to an inch above the top of the head. Take *profile* pictures of both sides of the head (left and right). Take a picture of the back of the head.

Again, these are not glamour shots. Take the pictures as the person normally appears, with or without makeup. Again, you can also include a set of photographs with glasses on and off, or with their hair up or down. You might end up with seven to eleven more facial pictures, but that is

CHAPTER 10: THE INDIVIDUAL PROTECTION PACKET

okay. Send the ones you want to your searchers and make sure the police have all of them.

The *background* should be plain and a light color, such as a flat wall. You can even hang a white bed sheet on a wall or door. You don't want a background that distracts from the picture or complicates reproductions. Use good lighting so that there are no shadows.

Then take a *full body* photograph of the front, both sides, and the back. Again, make sure the background is plain and a light color, such as a wall. Use good lighting.

You can also include close-up shots of any distinguishing features such as scars, tattoos, birthmarks, etc. Anything that will help identify you or your loved one. Title those photos as well.

Photo name: Mary JASON, Age 28, tattoo right wrist-1Apr2012

Photo name: John HENRY, age 15, scar on forehead-1April2012

Remember what I said about child custody cases, estranged spouses and other angry people. You may want to have photographs of them on file as well. That can include the video clips I'll describe below.

3. **Video clip/voice print**: Make two short video clips that can also be used as voice prints. Video clips can be produced using a camcorder, digital camera, or with a smartphone. One video clip should be fifteen seconds and the second, thirty seconds. This will be very useful for you and LE.

The video clip can also be used by the **media** to broadcast to the public and will have more of an impact than a simple photograph. It allows the audience to see your loved one's face and entire body (build). They can hear their voice and identify an accent and mannerisms.

More importantly, it is a personal and compelling *plea for help*. Your loved one's captor may also see this video on the television.

The detectives should arrange for two photographs (front and side facial) and both video clips (fifteen and thirty seconds) to be released to the media. They should also arrange for you, as the parents or spouse, to make a personal plea for help through the media. Discuss this tactic with your detective immediately. What if the police tell you that can be done later? Wrong! Time is of the essence. If they do not help with the arrangements, call the local television stations yourself. Take *advantage* of the media. It is your voice to your community and the world.

Crucial advice: If a loved one turns up missing, engage the media for assistance by giving them photographs and video clips, and by requesting a personal interview.

If you were watching television, which would you remember better, a single photograph of a missing person, or a short video clip of a person speaking to you and asking you for your assistance? Which would be more engaging or appealing? How about both!

The videos can be used to create **voice prints** that can be measured by special instruments and used for identification. There is even the capability of **facial recognition** by computers. Some people may dispute this technology, but it exists and is being perfected. If anything, this voice recording can be used by LEO to compare with future voice recordings, and they will find it very useful when interviewing witnesses and suspects. Again, LEO may need these video clips to produce *voice prints or a simple recording* for future comparisons.

If you are using a camera or smartphone without zoom capability, start with the person's face and then walk backwards until you have the full body in your screen, and then walk forward again.

CHAPTER 10: THE INDIVIDUAL PROTECTION PACKET

This is very important for producing a good video clip: use a light-colored simple background that will not distract from the person. Ensure you have good lighting to avoid shadows. Make sure there are not any background *noises* to interfere with producing a quality voice print. This can even include a humming noise in the background from an air conditioner or vehicle traffic.

Again, this is not a glamorous or professional movie. The person should dress and look normal. Just consider the background, shadows, and noises.

4. **Fingerprints**: Go to a local LE department or sheriff's office and ask for a complete set of fingerprints, also known as ten-prints (all ten fingers). If your local LE agencies do not help, check with your state police or the FBI. Ask for digital prints, also called *live scan fingerprinting*. If they do not have an *electronic fingerprinting machine*, ask for *ink prints*. However, please try to find a department that will provide electronically scanned fingerprints. You want at least four copies of the scanned fingerprint or the ink fingerprint.

Here is what happened to me once: I went for updated fingerprints for a security clearance. When the technician was finished, I could barely make out some of the fingerprints. Amazing! Make sure all the fingerprints are clear so that a fingerprint technician can read and categorize your fingerprints. If they are not clear, ask for another set.

You need professional prints, and it takes someone with experience to produce good prints where all the *friction ridges* can be properly read and *classified*. These ridges, or *patterns*, are called *loops, whorls,* and *arches*. The person taking the fingerprints must use a proper roll and make sure the print is not too dark, light, or smudged.

If the digital format is not available, ask for a complete set of ink prints. Again, you want at least four copies. I have seen fingerprints taken by experienced LEO that cannot be properly identified and categorized by the FBI.

The FBI's Integrated Automated Fingerprint Identification System (IAFIS) is the largest biometric database of fingerprints in the world. This system is used for criminals, security clearances, job applicants, and missing persons. Once fingerprints are entered into IAFIS, they can be electronically transferred and shared most anywhere in the world in minutes.

Keep four copies at home in a safe location. These digital or ink prints can also be scanned and uploaded onto your thumb drive. Set your scanner for high quality.

Here are some additional prints that always help investigators. In many cases, your local agency can take scanned or ink prints of a person's *full finger* (with all digits), as well as their *fingertips*, the *blade* (side) of their hand and *palm* prints. This requires a better (more expensive) electronic fingerprinting machine, or ink prints can be taken. It can be very valuable to have these additional prints available or on file.

Some hospitals will take *ink panels* (prints) of your baby's feet at birth. This includes the toes. These feet and toe ridges are called plantar surfaces, versus fingerprints, which are called palmar surfaces. Some hospitals no longer automatically take ink panels. You may have to *ask* the hospital to take these prints. Again, ask for four copies.

Babies generally start forming fingerprints after a few weeks, but it will not be easy taking their prints. Babies! They are not very good at listening when you tell them to let you roll the print. Yes, there is a technique to rolling good prints that can be properly classified. Get it done by a professional.

Caution! Many private organizations sponsor missing-children events where you can obtain fingerprints and a photo ID. There are also vendors

CHAPTER 10: THE INDIVIDUAL PROTECTION PACKET

who attend certain events and offer this service. Some commercial business provide something similar along with a mini-protection packet. This usually includes taking biographical information, making fingerprints, and producing a laminated identification card with photograph.

Sorry, but these mini-ID cards and commercial products are not good enough. Don't let them try to convince you otherwise. Remember, I said this is not a time to take shortcuts or leave out vital information. Everything we do is going to be first-rate. When I first begin exploring ways to protect our children and loved ones, I discovered the shortcomings and hazards of certain systems, so I decided to produce this book and the IPP system.

Second, who is talking all this information and what are they doing with this information? These businesses usually enter this information in a database in their personal computer to produce the mini-ID card. You do not want strangers having and keeping this information.

5. **Dental Records**: Ask your dentist for a complete set of *regular X-rays*, a *panograph X-ray*, and *bite impressions*. These records will be used for *dental forensics*. Explain to the dentist why you want these records, and he or she will know what to provide.

Most dentists take regular X-rays and bite impressions of their patients every year and a panograph typically every five years. You will need to update your children's IPP as their teeth change. For adults you will not have to update these records in your IPP unless there are significant changes—like most all your teeth fall out.

Again, these dental X-rays can be provided digitally. The dentist can e-mail digital copies to you or provide you with a digital copy you can scan into your computer. Make sure you ask for a "high-resolution" printout for making a good-quality scan to load on your thumb drive.

You can buy teeth-impression kits at most local pharmacies or purchase them online for $5 to $10. Read the directions carefully. You will be instructed to bite down on the card for several seconds and then place it in the sterile container or envelope provided. This bite impression will also retain the person's saliva for deoxyribonucleic acid, better known as DNA. Actually, it is not the saliva that provides the DNA. It is the skin (epithelial) cells that come from the mouth. Keep reading.

6. **DNA Buccal Swabs**: DNA buccal swab kits can be purchased from a local pharmacy or online. You can mail the swabs to a laboratory for analysis or you may be able to find a DNA laboratory in your local area. These kits are basically sterile Q-tips with a sterile container. *Buccal* means mouth or cheeks, by the way. Again, it is not really the saliva you are collecting, but the skin cells from inside the cheeks.

This is the least invasive and simplest method of collecting DNA (also called *reference samples*) for profiling by a forensics scientist or LE examiner. *DNA profiling* is also known as *genetic fingerprinting*.

The other collection methods are blood and other body fluids. Skin and hair samples can be used as long as the hair follicle is completely intact when the hair is extracted. The buccal method is just as reliable as any other sample, so go with the buccal swabs.

Some investigators say DNA profiles are not necessary. Wrong! Take the swabs and send them to the laboratory for analysis. A person's DNA may later be recovered from a number of locations and items. It will let the investigators know if it was in fact your loved one at a specific location or crime scene, such as the trunk of a car or a room within a particular house or other building. Your loved one's DNA may be found on the offender/attacker's body, proof that they are the guilty person. It can be found on pieces of clothing, rope, toothbrushes, Band-Aids, etc.

Now, you can simply store the swabs, but I highly recommend you have this DNA sample analyzed now. It can take several weeks, so have the results on hand and ready. Again, time is of the essence.

These DNA buccal swab kits can be purchased for $5 and the lab analysis will cost about $130. Follow the directions carefully. Generally, you will brush the swab inside a person's mouth for several seconds, firmly wiping inside both cheeks, collecting as many cells as possible. Remove the swab and then place it in a sterile container or envelope that comes with the kit. Yes, it may cost around $135 per person, but how much is your loved one worth?

7. **Medical Records**: Keep a personal copy of your medical records. This is just good practice for everyone. Take them with you when you *travel* or go on vacation. You can keep a copy of your dental records in this medical file as well. Think how valuable these records can be in the event you are away from home and have a medical emergency. We learned this in the Army, and most military members have a complete set of medical records and their shot records that they carry everywhere.

The medical records should identify any medical conditions, medicines, immunizations and shots, lab testing, treatment, etc. They may include X-rays.

Police *should* want to contact doctors, dentists, and other medical providers. Make sure they do! Not only can medical providers provide valuable information, but they can also become witnesses or suspects. Remember the case of Dr. Bradley?

8. **Iris Scan/Pictures**: An iris scan is arguably just as good as fingerprints for identifying a person. Certain biographical data, fingerprints, facial (recognition), and iris scans produce what is called *biometrics* identification.

An optometrist or ophthalmologist often takes pictures of the iris to check for medical conditions and diseases, such as glaucoma, macular degeneration, diabetes, high blood pressure, cancer, etc. These ocular photographs may be useful for identification, but are not the same as an electronic iris scan.

Iris scans are typically used by some law enforcement and national security agencies, but not many. Ask your local law enforcement department or a federal agency if they can take an iris scan to be kept on file. This is not likely, but is just a suggestion because technology and the uses of such scans advance with time.

Did I forget anything? You may have some good ideas yourself. I would like to keep stressing this point: it is very important for you to conduct your own research and learn as much as possible for the various reasons expressed. Doing your own research helps you retain all this information. It clarifies certain questions you may have or may have missed. The more you learn, the smarter you become about security. The smarter you are, the safer you become. You are your family's guardian and protector. No shortcuts, okay?

Let's move on to the most important part of your Individual Protection Packet—the Biographical Form. This is the crucial *checklist* for both you and the police. It is the *lifeline* to being found quickly.

Don't forget to prepare missing person posters and keep them on your computer. Of course you will include their name, nickname, and full description. Include a front and profile picture of the face and a full-body picture. You can add a picture of their car and license plate. Make-up a variety of posters and keep them updated.

Chapter 11

BIOGRAPHICAL FORM

The following information can be typed or handwritten. Preferably, type this information and save it on your computer to be updated and added to your flash (thumb) drive. If it is handwritten, then scan it and add to your IPP on your computer and thumb drive. Please make sure it is legible to avoid any mistakes. If you make a mistake, just line it out and make the correction.

Save the computer file the same way you will save the e-mail, by using the person's first and last name, followed by their age, IPP, and the date you saved or updated the file.

Example: Elizabeth SMITH, 22, IPP-10Oct11

Please write the number and question for each line and then provide your answer. This will assist the detectives with their references and reports. Add as much detail as possible.

When you see the line for "Clothes," think to yourself, what does my loved one commonly wear? Keep in mind that the police officer or detective will ask you what your loved one was wearing the last time they were seen. However, it helps to know what kind of clothes your loved one typically buys and wears if they are a runaway or kidnapped by a family member. Do they dress casually in jeans, T-shirts, and tennis shoes, or do they dress preppy or formal?

When describing colors, explain if the color is light, medium, or dark; for example, dark brown hair or light blue eyes. Skin tones can be light, medium, or dark, and skin complexions can be smooth or rough. You can describe a mild or severe form of acne, which can be on the face or on the body.

When you answer any of the questions, think like a detective. Give the question some thought. Be very thorough when answering all of these questions. Use additional sheets if necessary.

For bank accounts and debit/credit cards, do *not* include bank and credit card numbers. This applies to gasoline and store credit cards as well. The police/detectives only need to know the name on the account(s) and the bank or financial institution. They will need the same information for other credit cards, e.g., Target, Discover, Exxon, etc. They will issue a subpoena to the bank or company. If they need the account number, they can ask you.

If you have a POC for the banks and other cards, you can always include their names and numbers. This way the detective can easily and quickly contact them. We know our branch bank manager and her main number. Monitoring the use of credit cards is a quick way to locate a missing person. Not only will the location and exact time be identified, but there may be a video as well. Who is on that video may be telling.

Remember, you can add or take away anything from this list. You may have some better ideas. The point is to provide the police and detectives with as much information as possible. They may need to share this information

CHAPTER 11: BIOGRAPHICAL FORM

with other agencies across the country. They will keep it confidential, so don't let this be a concern.

1. FIRST & LAST NAME/AGE: (For quick reference)

2. DATE BIOGRAPHICAL SHEET LAST UPDATED:

3. PERSON'S FULL LEGAL NAME:

4. MAIDEN NAME:

5. NICKNAMES USED:

6. OTHER NAMES USED:

7. POINTS OF CONTACT FOR NOTIFICATIONS & INFORMATION: (Parents and guardians.

  Please include physical addresses where they live. Include all telephone numbers, and indicate the type, and all e-mail addresses.)

8. DATE OF BIRTH: (Spell out the month)

9. PLACE OF BIRTH: (City/county/state/country)

10. SOCIAL SECURITY NUMBER(S):

11. CITIZENSHIP(S)/NATIONALITY:

12. RACE (ethnicity) and SEX (gender):

13. RELIGION:

14. HEIGHT and WEIGHT:

15. BUILD: (Tall, medium, short, slim, medium, heavy)

16. EYES: (Color (along with light or dark), contacts, glasses/reading or distance)

17. HAIR: (Color, natural or dyed, length, style)

18. LANGUAGES: (And levels of comprehension)

19. PASSPORT NUMBER & PLACE OF ISSUE, WITH ISSUE & EXPIRATION DATES: (Make a clear copy of first two pages with picture and information. Scan this to your thumb drive.)

20. OTHER IDENTIFICATION (ID#) NUMBERS: (Government, employee, school, etc.)

21. CURRENT DRIVER'S LICENSE NUMBER and STATE:

22. PREVIOUS DRIVER'S LICENSE NUMBER(S) and STATE(S):

23. SKIN COMPLEXION: (Light, medium, dark, olive, smooth, rough, acne)

24. CLOTHES **TYPICALLY WORN** & CARRIED: (Sizes are important)

25. JEWLERY & ACCESSORIES TYPICALLY CARRIED: (Description of jewelry, purses, etc.)

26. **CELL PHONE,** PAGERS, ETC.: (Numbers, carriers, locations purchased)

27. **E-MAIL** ADDRESSES: (Include personal, work, Twitter, blog names, etc.)

CHAPTER 11: BIOGRAPHICAL FORM

28. **FAVORITE PLACE**(S) MOST LIKELY TO BE: (Friend, mall, store, etc.)

29. RECORDS ON FILE & WHERE: (Checklist)

30. MEDICAL X-RAYS:

31. DENTAL X-RAYS:

32. OPTOMETRIST: (Include prescription)

33. FINGERPRINTS:

34. BABY FOOTPRINTS:

35. PHOTOGRAPHS:

36. DNA SAMPLE:

37. PERSONAL BIOGRAPHICAL SHEET:

38. FLASH (thumb) DRIVE or CD/DVD LAST UPDATED:

39. ALL **IDENTIFIERS**: (Glasses, contacts and colors, braces, hearing aids, wigs/weaves worn, facial hair, deformities, limps, twitches, scars, moles, tattoos, piercings, birthmarks, etc.)

40. **CHARACTERISTICS** & MANNERISMS: (Speech, hearing, behavior, unique walking/standing/sitting mannerisms, soft/loud spoken, outgoing/shy, stands erect/slumped, eye contact, smile, dimples, etc.)

41. **HOBBIES**: (Groups, sports, hiking, running, cars, music, movies, cooking, books, etc.)

42. SPECIAL **LIKES & DISLIKES**: (Clubs, dancing, food, drinks, reading, clubs)

43. ALL **KNOWN ADDRESSES**, CURRENT & PAST/LOCATIONS: (Home, work, school, sports, day care, special functions, playgrounds, past favorite/hiding places, theaters, restaurants, libraries, etc.)

44. CURRENT HOME ADDRESS:

45. PRIOR HOME ADDRESS:

46: ALL OTHER ADDRESSES:

47. **ALL CONTACTS (Past & Current)**: Other RELATIVES (Parents, siblings, grandparents, uncle/aunts, etc.), BOY/GIRL FRIENDS, CLOSE FRIENDS, NEIGHBORHOOD FRIENDS, SCHOOL FRIENDS, ROOMMATES, KNOWN ACQUAINTANCES, BABYSITTERS: (Names, addresses & all contact information)

48. MOTHER'S FULL NAME and DOB:

49. ALL STEPMOTHERS' FULL NAMES and DOBs:

50. FATHER'S FULL NAME and DOB:

51. ALL STEPFATHERS' FULL NAMES and DOBs:

52. SPOUSE'S FULL NAME and DOB:

53. FORMER SPOUSE(s)' FULL NAME(s) and DOB(s):

54. SIGNIFICANT OTHER'S FULL NAME and DOB:

CHAPTER 11: BIOGRAPHICAL FORM

55. ALL FORMER SIGNIFICANT OTHERS' FULL NAMES and DOBs:

56: ALL BROTHERS' FULL NAMES and DOBs (Include stepbrothers):

57. ALL SISTERS' FULL NAMES and DOBs (Include stepsisters):

58. ALL OTHER RELATIVES:

59. All POSSIBLE **HOSTILE PERSONS** & WHY: (Family members, relatives, boy/girlfriends, neighbors, friends, roommates, online acquaintances, people at work, school, sports, hangouts, etc.) Find or get photographs of these individuals. Find out where they live. A private investigator can complete a quick portfolio on these people in a few short hours. Some PI's like to do this online. That's okay, but they need to physically verify the information and take photographs and short video clips.

60. **MEDICAL** CONTACTS & HISTORY: (Doctors, nurses, clinics, hospitals, dentists, optometrists (eye), illnesses/conditions, allergies, medications, etc.)

61. ALL **TRANSPORTATION**: (Vehicles owned or used, vehicles used by friends, buses, trains, planes, rental cars, etc. Include online club memberships.)

62. ALL **BANKS** & CREDIT CARDS: (Do *not* include account numbers here.)

63. **POLICE & COURT** MATTERS/RECORDS: (Criminal, civil, juvenile, family services, etc.) Are there any past or court; child custody issues, domestic violence, arrests, etc.?

64. PASTE PHOTOGRAPHS: (Facial, full body, and identify features.)

Reduce these photos to approximately 2 inches x 2 inches. Update photos as needed. It was mentioned above to identify vehicles and license plates. You can include pictures of these vehicles as well.

Okay, that's it. We have been over this, but one more time for good measure.

If a loved one turns up missing, contact the local authorities immediately and then contact one of the national agencies as well. Listen! Contact *both* the local police and the national agencies (NCMEC or LBTH) at the same time if you feel it is necessary. You can also contact the FBI and the other federal agencies as well. Discuss this with the detective. Start a journal and write down everyone you contact and everything that is happening.

Remember, do not let anyone tell you there is a twenty-four-hour waiting period. Explain why you think your loved one is in fact missing, if it is not obvious. Some police officers may feel a missing teenager or adult is a runaway. Well, they could be wrong. Your loved one could be involved in an *accident* or they could have been *abducted*. Who knows? Time is of the essence.

Even most law enforcement officers agree that the first few hours are the most critical time in which to recover a missing person. If you are not successful in getting their attention, ask to speak with a supervisor or contact another LE department.

Many businesses have contingency plans for locating missing children and adults. As explained, these include department stores, schools, day-care centers, and homes for the elderly. If your child cannot be found in a store or the mall, contact the police immediately. Then contact the store manager and mall security. Ask them about their "Code Adam" program.

When a LEO or security arrives on the scene, be prepared to answer their questions (start thinking), and provide them with your Individual

Protection Packet (IPP). What were they wearing? Who were they with? Did you see anything suspicious that day? Hand them that IPP thumb drive and text them the photographs and video clip on your smartphone or computer. Give them a photograph if that is what you have.

Send that text message to everyone you know. Same with an e-mail. You can use the photos to create a poster. Make hundreds of copies and hand them out if that is what you decide to do.

Let the LEO know if your loved one has a cellular telephone that can be used to electronically track his/her whereabouts. Hopefully you decided to buy and use a personal GPS tracker. Wouldn't that be nice? You can also give them the bank and credit card information, so alerts can be established.

Don't try to second guess or withhold information that may be crucial to the police or detectives. Is your child involved in a custody battle? Is there an abusive relationship? Are they associated with a gang? Be truthful and tell the police everything up front. Don't let embarrassment get in the way. Let the police decide what is important and unimportant.

You can decide to hire a private investigator. I would! Remember, many law enforcement departments have manpower and resource limitations. They may also be restricted by legal, jurisdictional, and departmental regulations. Discuss this matter with the detective.

Know that there are specialized *search teams* that assist LEO using highly trained search dogs and trained volunteers. Ask the police officer if their department or office has search dogs or search teams. Ask them if their agency has access to private or civilian search teams.

Make sure the detectives effectively use the media. Get your loved one's pictures and video clip on the television as fast as possible. You may decide to contact the media and make a personal plea as well. These two steps should be accomplished in the first twenty-four hours. Not days or weeks later.

Chapter 12

ABBREVIATED - INDIVIDUAL PROTECTION PACKET

As mentioned earlier, businesses and organizations can take important steps to protect their customers and members, and to prevent lawsuits for negligence or liability. It is called **due diligence** and **risk management**.

Schools, churches, day-care centers, and assisted living facilities can take safety precautions. Why not? Why wouldn't you? This is especially important if you are taking students, customers, or members on organized field trips or vacations, especially foreign travel.

Before I go on, remember I mentioned **workplace violence**. This is another serious issue and topic. If you are the owner, manager, or supervisor of a business, you must learn more about workplace violence and take steps to prevent acts of violence by both employees and customers. This also includes protecting your employees when they arrive and leave work. Put up some lights and erect visible CCTV cameras around the property.

This is an abbreviated version of the Individual Protection Packet and Biographical Form. Fill out the forms and collect the following information. Decide what information you want to collect and what steps you want to take for an effective security program.

Some people feel these steps create anxiety and alarm. Others will see it as being cautious and smart. Do not risk someone else's safety and life by being naïve or careless.

When taking the photographs, be prepared for an argument. Many teenagers and chaperones will not want their pictures taken. Vanity (foolish pride)! Just let them know the pictures are confidential and will not be shared with anyone. Reassure them that the pictures will be deleted and destroyed after the trip.

Take **photographs** as described above, but you do not have to take them all. The first photograph will be the full-body shot. Have the person hold up a homemade place card that simply provides their full name. This can be used with the full length front shot, so it doesn't look like a mug shot. Again, the card will not be needed for the additional photographs.

If you are following the guidelines in the previous chapter, take a minimum of four photographs: the facial shot and the full length shots from the front and either side. Just imagine how valuable these photographs will be at a busy theme park or in a foreign country.

The chaperones can take a picture of each child in their group to save to their cell phones. This also applies to children at school and day care centers, as well as elderly people at assisted living facilities and hospitals. Use your imagination.

An **Emergency Identification Card** should always be carried by everyone. Chaperones, staff, and other points of contact will need to be added to the emergency telephone numbers. Don't forget to include all the other information listed above. At a minimum, write everything down on a sheet of paper and have the person fold it up and put it in their pocket or purse.

CHAPTER 12: ABBREVIATED - INDIVIDUAL PROTECTION PACKET

Fingerprints are a very valuable tool. If you can convince the person, or parents/guardians, get a set of ten prints and have them available. They can be returned at the end of the trip.

Most organizations obtain a **Liability Release Form** that is signed by all parties. This is good advice, but remember that the form is not going to protect anyone unless due diligence is exercised. However, please keep in mind that this security plan is not about legal issues; it is about saving someone's life.

Medical Authorization Forms are a necessity. Most hospitals and clinics will not provide treatment or administer certain medicines for juveniles or unconscious patients without written authorization. These forms should be legally notarized by the parents and guardians. Again, emergency points of contact can be added to this form and should include all available telephone numbers and e-mail addresses.

Just remember that the police and other authorities need certain information to initiate a *successful* search and rescue as *quickly* as possible. This is the minimal suggested information that should be on this modified biographical form.

If you prefer, type up a form and insert lines where the information can be hand printed. Make sure the instructions include "write legibly."

Scan this form along with all other forms and photographs to several secure thumb drives and pass them out to the primary chaperones or staff. Don't forget to include photographs, or even a video clip, on two or more cell phones carried by the chaperones.

1. FIRST & LAST NAME/AGE: (For quick reference)
2. PERSON'S FULL LEGAL NAME:
3. OTHER NAMES USED: (Identify if maiden name, nickname, or former name)
4. HOME ADDRESS: (Where they live, not just a mailing address)

5. PERSONAL CELL PHONE NUMBER(S):
6. PAGERS AND OTHER PERSONAL DEVICES:
7. PERSONAL E-MAIL ADDRESS(ES):
8. EMERGENCY POINTS OF CONTACT: (Parents and guardians. Include all telephone numbers by type and all e-mail addresses.)
9. DATE OF BIRTH: (Spell out month/day/year):
10. CITIZENSHIP(S) / NATIONALITY:
11. SEX (gender) and RACE (ethnicity):
12. HEIGHT and WEIGHT:
13. BUILD: (Tall, medium, short, slim, heavy)
14. EYES: (Color (along with light or dark), contacts, glasses/reading or distance)
15. HAIR: (Color, natural or dyed, length, style)
16. SKIN COMPLEXION: (Light, medium, dark, olive, smooth, rough, acne)
17. LANGUAGES: (And levels of comprehension)
18. PASSPORT NUMBER & PLACE OF ISSUE WITH ISSUE & EXPIRATION DATES: (Make a clear copy of first two pages with picture and information.)
19. ALL **IDENTIFIERS**: (Glasses, contacts and colors, braces, hearing aids, wigs/weaves worn, facial hair, dimples, deformities, limps, twitches, scars, moles, tattoos, piercings, birthmarks, etc.)
20. **CHARACTERISTICS** & MANNERISMS: (Speech, hearing, behavior, unique walking/standing/sitting mannerisms, soft/loud spoken, outgoing/shy, stands erect/slumped, eye contact, smile, etc.)
21. **MEDICAL** CONTACTS & HISTORY: (Doctors, nurses, clinics, hospitals, dentists, optometrists (eye), illnesses/conditions, allergies, medications, etc.)

Chapter 13

BASIC RULES TO FOLLOW

I have taken the various suggestions listed in chapter 2 and added them here as basic rules to follow, and I've also included more valuable information. For your children and teenagers, you may very well want to tell them "These are our rules!" But these suggestions and rules are not absolute. Decide what steps you want to take. You may have some new and better ideas.

Children and teenagers need rules and they need boundaries. More importantly, they need protection, and that is our responsibility. And this does not apply just to children and teenagers. Some adults are not very responsible and mature. They may need a few rules as well.

Keep in mind that while I say "home," these suggestions can apply most anywhere: at home, your business, place of work, school, and any other location you and your loved ones frequent or visit.

One last thing before we get started: don't forget what you have learned. You need to protect yourself and your loved ones from these violent offenders and sexual predators. You need to protect yourselves from the possibility of a home invasion or attacks by street gangs and other criminal elements. Listen, home invasions happen every day. Gang attacks happen every day, and these attacks can be very spontaneous. These are very violent offenders. You need to be aware of your surroundings. Be alert and be prepared.

Rule 1: IPP - Complete an Individual Protection Packet on yourself and each of your loved ones. This includes the Biographical Form. Keep them updated. Take your thumb drive with you at all times, so you can use it and so you can hand it over to the police immediately.

You may need to make several thumb drives to keep at home and work. Make sure each parent has a copy. Give a copy to another relative or friend. Use secure thumb drives so you can protect this information. Remember, the intent is to give the police and investigators everything they need, so they can act quickly and have all the information they could possibly need access to.

The only problem with keeping these Biographical Forms on the computer or in your e-mail system is the possibility of being hacked. If you have an Internet security system and you use strong secure passwords, you will probably be okay. It is very important that everyone use good passwords and that they change their passwords from time to time. Just write them down and hide them somewhere near your computer for easy access.

Rule 2: Emergency Identification Cards - Make several E-IDC for your entire family and keep them with you at all times. Keep copies in the glove box and center console of all your vehicles. Keep these cards updated as well.

Rule 3: Strangers - Under no circumstances should you meet with a stranger alone or without someone knowing the circumstances and details.

This applies to Internet dating and blind dates, and any other social or business meeting, including parties. If you want privacy, consider having a friend drop by for a quick introduction. This will put any would-be attacker on notice that there is now a witnesses. The other option is to let someone know where you are going and with whom. Just make a quick phone call upon arrival and when you leave. Make it a quick and casual phone call. Again, this will put any would-be attacker on notice.

If you have a friend join you or just drop in for a few minutes, have your friend ask a few personal questions. That takes you off that awkward hook. Your friend can ask most anything—like where they work and where they live. They might even ask their birthday and what kind of car they drive. Your friend will be leaving, so you can just laugh it off after they depart. If this bothers your date, then perhaps this is not someone you want to be around. Really, who would care, other than someone who is nervous or has something to hide?

Rule 4: Personal Information - Do NOT provide strangers with personal identification information over the telephone or in person unless you absolutely trust them. Always know who you are talking to and in most cases verify who they are.

This personal identification information includes your full name, home address, telephone numbers, date of birth and/or Social Security Number. What pieces of information you don't give someone, they can probably find on the Internet and through public records. Give someone certain pieces of that information, and they can come visit you at your home in a matter of hours.

Internet and social networks such as Facebook, MySpace, dating services, dating parties, etc. can be dangerous and are hunting grounds for predators. Do NOT put your address, telephone numbers, and date of birth on social pages. You can give this information to who you want when they ask. Why plaster it all over the Internet without a good reason? Most anyone can hack your social page. If you want birthday wishes, then change the day and year by one or two figures.

Crucial Advice: Why would your bank, any other financial institution, or another company you do business with call you and ask for your personal information that they already have on file? Ask them that question. The same goes for e-mails. No bank or financial institution would ever send you an e-mail asking for this information. Remember, identify theft is growing by leaps and bounds.

A suggestion for verifying someone's identity over the telephone is to ask them for their name (first and last), company or business name, city and state, telephone contact numbers, and contact e-mail address. Write everything down of course. Ask them for both their *main* number and *direct* number. Many company and government representatives have an employee identification number. Ask for that employee identification number. This is the reason for that number: customer complaints, safety, and security. If someone refuses to identify themselves and provide any of this information, I would ask them, "Why not?"

Tell them you will call back in five to ten minutes after you verify who they are. They will understand this. After hanging up the phone, Google all the information you have written down and see if everything matches up.

You can also call the main number and asked to be patched through to the caller. Listen closely to what the receptionist/operator says when answering the phone, to include any background noises. Does the person answering the phone sound legitimate? Did the transfer sound real? Playing detective can be fun.

As far as your mail or other correspondence, make sure you take a hard pen and scratch out sensitive information, for example your DOB, SSN, and account numbers. Then tear the paper up into small pieces and throw it away. *Preferably*, use a quality paper shredder. A good paper shredder cuts the paper in a cross pattern, so the strips cannot be reconstructed. Cheap shredders will not last very long. Buy one that can shred multiple pages, and do not exceed the recommended number of pages in order to prevent burning out the motor. If the shredder can shred five to ten pages at a time, only shred half that number.

CHAPTER 13: BASIC RULES TO FOLLOW

Keep your identification cards, credit cards, important documents and even your checkbooks in a safe place at home. Preferably a secured safe. This even includes password cheat sheets. There is no reason to carry your social security card, passport, multiple credit cards, etc. with you unless you know they will be needed.

Rule 5: Strangers at the door - Do NOT open your door to strangers and do not invite them into your home—even if someone is at home with you. The other person(s) in the house can become victims as well. It has actually happened.

When you have a stranger who shows up on your doorstep, tell them very politely, with a smile, to wait a minute. Close the door and lock it. Consider installing a peep hole or a voice transmitter for stronger security. Door chains are useless unless they are heavy duty and installed properly.

Crucial advice: Never ever let your children answer the door alone. Make them aware of "**stranger danger**."

If a stranger unexpectedly shows up at your door, call a neighbor or friend and let them know what is going on. Keep them on the other line and carry the phone with you to the door. If you have a home alarm with a remote key FOB, carry that to the door with you and keep your finger on the panic button.

You can also call the police if you feel the least bit suspicious or nervous. Remember, ALWAYS trust your instincts. I cannot emphasize that comment enough. Most people have very good instincts. Trust them. Don't worry about appearing silly or being embarrassed. Some strangers may appear irritated by the inconvenience, but so what? They are strangers. If you explain you are just being cautious, they will understand. If not, so what?

I am a big supporter of personal and home defense. Everyone, especially women, should carry or have a weapon, to include a gun, mace, and/or a stun gun. Even your car keys grasped in your hand with one key sticking out can be a defense weapon. An air horn (can) might help. However, I do *not* recommend relying on your ability to fight back with your hands and feet only. Even men can lose that fight against a determined and stronger attacker. Having said that, if you do have to fight, fight and scream with all your fury, and don't stop fighting.

Why? According to official reports and a study, an estimated 683,000 women are forcibly raped every year. That's 1,871 per day or one every 1.3 minutes. Thousands of burglaries and robberies occur every day as well. Strangers at your door pose a problem. Look out your window. If they are wearing a FedEx uniform and there is a big FedEx truck parked out front, then you might be okay. I said, "might."

After you have made your phone call to notify someone of your situation, when you reopen the door, step outside and close the door behind you. Preferably, you should lock the door behind you. If you do, don't forget your key! You should have your phone or remote FOB with you. Ask the person for their company identification card. If you feel safe, invite the person inside or remain outside. I do both.

I recently saw a new remote door viewer with camera and intercom. It is fairly small, and you can just slip it over the top of the door. No assembly required. When someone approaches the door, you receive an alert. You can actually see and talk to them over the remote system linked to your smartphone or laptop. Even if you are not at home, you can still talk to them over the intercom and make them *think* you are at home. Tell them are you are busy if you want.

You need to think of all these options and decide what you are going to do. Discuss this with your family and come up with rules for the house.

Remember what I said earlier. You do not have to become paralyzed or consumed by fear, but you should be smart and use that fear. Take certain security precautions or steps to protect yourself and your family. Do not worry about embarrassment. Your safety is more important.

Rule 6: Secluded and dark areas - Avoid encounters and confrontations with strangers in secluded and/or dark areas.

Be on alert, be confident, and be very observant of what is going on around you. Alert! Confident! Observant! The more you look around, the more you will see, and the more you will know. Awareness and prevention! It also scares would-be attackers to notice that you are being observant and confident. They prefer "soft targets" (easy) over "hard targets" (difficult).

What do you do if you are in a dark parking lot at night and a stranger approaches you, or "appears" to be approaching you? Remember, they are cunning. What do you do? Hit the panic button on your remote key FOB. Carry a personal alert device with you. Pull out that mace or stun gun. Run or scream. Don't feel silly or be embarrassed. It is all about *survival*, staying alive.

Remember what I said about alarms and personal defense. Another option is to carry something in your hand. You can carry your car FOB in your hand and have your finger on the panic button. Go ahead and push it once or twice before you reach your car. That will attract some attention or possibly scare off a would-be attacker. If you do not have a key FOB, carry a personal alert device or a can air horn.

You can carry your car keys in your hand. Place a key in your palm and close your hand making a fist. Keep one key sticking out like a knife. This makes an excellent self-defense weapon. If you are attacked, always go for the eyes and the face. Start *stabbing* as fast as possible. Stabs are faster and more effective than slashes. Scream and stab and don't give up. Assailants twice the size of the victim have been known to flee when someone starts to fight back.

If you buy mace, do not think it is just something you point and spray. Do your research. Read up on the different types of mace and how to use them. Read the directions that come with your package. Buy a few refills and use one for training. Draw a face on a sheet of paper and tack that piece of paper to a tree. Spray that piece of paper from different distances, say three and six feet. Always think about splash-back and the wind. What about the laws in your state?

In addition to the typical spray canister, **Kimber makes the Pepper Blaster** that looks and handles a little bit like a gun. Aim and pull the trigger. The pepper spray is delivered at a powerful ninety mph to hit the target fast and avoid back spray. I have seen small metal cylinders that attach to a key ring and deliver one to two bursts. Like the stun gun in the flashlight, I'm sure there are flashlights with pepper spray.

Did you know a lot of criminals practice spraying themselves and each other, so they learn how to fight and function when sprayed with mace? They don't become immune to the mace; they just learn how to ignore the effects and continue their attack.

Stun guns are legal in many states and are an effective personal defense weapon. Call your local police and find out. Remember, call more than once source. Not everyone is right. Do not practice on yourself or others. This may sound funny, but it has been done. If you purchase a stun gun, then treat it like all other weapons. Learn how it works and learn safety. Learn about the laws in your state and in other states if you carry the stun gun with you.

Crucial advice: Remember this simple reasoning: if someone is crazy enough to break into your home, they may be crazy enough to hurt you.

Why is someone breaking into your home? Is it to steal valuables, or are they looking to rape or kill you or your loved ones? Will they allow a witness to live?

If you don't like guns and you are totally opposed to them, then skip the next several paragraphs. Yes, in America you are allowed to own and possess a firearm in your home. Some people think it is not allowed. However, there may be restrictions on carrying a weapon on your person or in your car, or having a firearm in your place of work. Learn the laws in your state.

In some states you can carry a weapon in your car under certain conditions. They may include having the weapon locked in one container or compartment and having the ammunition locked in a separate container or compartment. Laws vary from state to state. In some states you can carry a shotgun or rifle in the cab unsecured as long as it is not loaded. Find out!

If you are going to carry a gun on your person, make sure you have a Concealed Carry Weapon (CCW) license\permit, which includes certain background checks and professional training. The training you receive when getting your carry permit is not enough training. In fact, in some states the training is downright irresponsible.

Whatever you do, make sure you know how to use the gun, and that includes both shooting and safety.

Anyone carrying a gun should have had hours and hours and hours of professional training, to include both firearm techniques and safety. Both are very, very crucial. Before carrying a hand gun, you should have completed a professional firearms course and shot at the target range on no less than two to four occasions. This range qualification should include firing a few hundred rounds through that gun using different shooting techniques.

You also need to practice both your loading techniques and your drawing techniques at the range. This is all part of your overall safety training. If you carry your weapon in a purse, handbag, or belly bag, then practice drawing from your purse or bags. If you carry a handgun in an ankle holster, practice drawing from that holster. Gun training should be as strict as getting a driver's license. You should take it just as seriously. Study and train.

I like the Taurus Judge handgun for home defense. It holds only five cartridges, but those rounds can include .410 shotgun shells and .45

caliber bullets. Believe it or not, certain models of the Judge are easy for women and smaller people to shoot. The recoil is not as bad as some think.

With this weapon you can load the first three or four chambers with .410 shotgun shells and the last one or two with .45 caliber bullets. Or, use all shotgun shells and have a back-up handgun. Your choice. When firing through bedroom doorways, hallways, or large rooms, the pellets (and discs) will spread out into a wide pattern of two to four inches. This makes it easier to hit someone, as opposed to hoping that tiny bullet strikes its intended target. The pellets and discs inside the .410 shotgun shell will not penetrate doors and walls and travel through to other rooms.

This is why you should also use hollow-point bullets. They expand when they hit something solid and usually they will not penetrate people and walls. Hollow-points expand once they hit and enter something. Should they penetrate, they will be flattened and not have as much velocity (speed/power). Most states allow hollow points, but check with your local law enforcement department to make sure. And never take one person's word as gospel. Call a couple of departments or agencies. Google it on your computer: "What are the gun laws in Florida?" Make sure the information you are reading is current. The Internet often contains outdated material. Go to an official website for your law enforcement department. That may be your state's Department of Justice.

Like any of us, individual police officers and lawyers are not always correct. This comes from someone with thirty-eight years in the business of law enforcement, investigations, and private security. Do your research. Always verify information through multiple sources.

Know this: each state has different laws pertaining to *concealed carry permits* and the *use of private firearms* by citizens. The laws for carrying a concealed weapon on your person are different than carrying a weapon in your car or having one in your home or business. What is a weapon? There are also different laws pertaining to protecting yourself in your home verses your business and car. Many states have gone to the *Castle Doctrine* that gives you more legal rights in your home, or in all three places. Know what all these laws are.

There has been a lot of controversy over the "stand your ground" law in Florida and other states. This applies to individuals who are authorized to carry a weapon in public, either openly or concealed. Know those laws as well. I attended a private firearm course, so I could obtain a concealed carry permit. I was both shocked and scared by the level of instruction and some of the people who were allowed to pass this course. It was evident to me the firearms instructor only wanted to pass people and collect the money. Most states need stronger training requirements for citizens to be allowed to carry weapons in public. Most firearms instructors need to be more strict and not fear telling someone they failed the course.

Speaking of self-defense, there are short courses a person can take for close-quarter fighting or hand-to hand combat. Some are designed specifically for women and children. Some courses last several hours and are broken up over nights or weekends. They might be broken down into various levels. A very famous style is the **Krav Maga technique**. There are instructors in various schools in most cities, and there are traveling instructors. You don't have to spend thousands of hours or dollars. Just go get several hours of training and learn how to hit or kick someone where it will stop them. There are other mixed martial arts programs available for learning limited self-defense. Make it a family affair. Google, *"krav maga"* or *"self-defense techniques."* To find a qualified instructor in your area.

Rule 7: Being followed - Be very aware of someone following you in your car, both day and night. Of course, being followed on foot can be just as important. This includes inside parking lots, on sidewalks, and even inside a mall or other building. I will address being followed while driving for the most part, but apply the same principles and techniques to walking or arriving home or at work. Yes, these cunning criminals have been known to hide at your home and wait until you exit your car or unlock your house door to attack.

I can follow you for hours and days, and you will never know I am there. Most criminals have some talent for physical surveillance, but they get anxious and tend to follow too closely. However, most people are not trained in counter-surveillance and do not think to see if they are being followed. Vehicle and foot surveillance is a very common tactic used by rapists and serial killers. Many criminals receive training in surveillance and attack techniques. Their school is called prison and gangs.

Glance in your review mirror or look behind you on occasion. You should be doing this already as part of defensive driving. I teach others to look in their review mirrors and both side mirrors constantly as they are driving. Before changing lanes you should "glance" at all three mirrors and then glance over your left or right shoulder by quickly turning your head. Do not depend on your mirrors alone.

If you see the same car or driver several times, you may want to take action. If this does happen, do NOT panic. Remain calm and THINK. Just take a few deep breaths and tell yourself you are going to handle this situation. Why did I say take a few deep breaths? When some people become nervous or scared they will unknowingly hold their breath. This causes you to become a little bit dizzy because you are not getting all your normal oxygen. BREATHE and THINK.

If you think you are being followed, do not drive to your neighborhood or house. You don't want them to know where you live. Ride around and see if the car continues to follow you. Turn into a parking lot with *multiple exits* where there are a lot of people and lights. Don't get yourself cornered. You don't have to be sneaky or covert; let the person following you know that you are on to them. Drive up to a gas station and start blowing your horn. That will cause other people or the attendant to look around. In any situation, always attract as much attention as possible. Again, be careful. Hopefully they will leave. Don't take any chances.

Try to stop somewhere safe and call the police. Give the police a description of both the car and the driver. Hopefully, you can get a license-plate number. Remember, I said not to panic. Take a few deep breaths of air and start thinking. Look carefully at the car and driver. Look for anything noticeable or distinguishing about both. This can be damage to the car, or stickers on the bumper or windows. It can be the color of the paint or the condition of the paint job. Can you distinguish anything about the driver? Male or female? Their approximate age? What about the color or length of their hair?

A good thing about cell phones is they have cameras and voice recorders. If your memory is not very good, you can also use your phone's recorder to describe information as you see it happening. I have to write down everything and I'm not going to do that when I'm driving, so I use a personal mini-recorder I purchased. But I can also use the voice recorder application on my smartphone. When I do not have my cameras available, I use my cell phone to take pictures of license plates and house numbers. Sometimes I see posters for events and will snap a picture for later.

You read additional information in an earlier chapter about criminals and predators posing as LEOs. Go back and read this part again. In April 2012, a police imposter stopped several cars in North Carolina. In some cases he robbed them. He managed to elude police for months. At the same time, a police impersonator in Nevada kidnapped a woman and raped her. There are many of these cases.

Crucial advice: Whatever option(s) you choose, always be very careful that you are paying attention to your driving and your surroundings at the same time. Do not develop *tunnel vision* or have an *accident.*

Rule 8: Alarm system - Seriously consider buying an alarm system for your home along with the monitoring service. I use and recommend ADT security services.

Alarm systems and services are no longer that expensive. Just be careful that the sales person does not try to oversell equipment for your home.

If you get an alarm system, ask for two or three remote FOBs. They are easier than using the main key pad inside your house. The main alarm console and FOB should also have panic buttons.

You do want an alarm for your garage doors. Again, many of the door and window sensors are connected by radio frequency (RF), and you no longer have to hard wire all the contacts to the main box.

You can also get smoke and gas detectors that will be monitored by the alarm company. The technology is advancing by the years. Some are now directly connected with medical alert, and monitors can listen in to hear if there is a problem. Not sure I care for that option! Soon they will tell you to change your socks.

Ask for a couple of alarm warning signs to place in the front and back of your house. Maybe even on the sides. You can also ask for the smaller window stickers. I have them on all my doors and windows on the first floor.

Like I described in chapter 2, you can also purchase other home security equipment at certain stores and online. I keep saying "at home," but all of this applies to home, business, and car.

Want a back-up alarm system? We all know *a good dog can be a very effective deterrent*. I trained security dog is even more effective.

CCTV/Security cameras: I am going to suggest the Closed Circuit Television (CCTV) security cameras and security systems. As you read earlier, these cameras can be strategically placed around the home, inside and out. These systems can be monitored over your computer, laptop, or cell phone from anywhere. They can include low light or nighttime (full dark) capability. You can have them professionally installed or buy self-installation kits with anywhere from two to six cameras, or more. They are also available in hard wire or RF.

You can also purchase the portable audio/visual monitors I mentioned. Just place them in certain rooms and you can watch the recording later or over your laptop or cell phone. Some of the monitors also have a remote camera you can swivel back and forth.

Rule 9: Personal GPS Device - Without a doubt, buy GPS personal trackers for your children and loved ones. You will also need to buy the monitoring service for your cell phone or computer. I recommend Brick House Security for this equipment and other items.

The devices and service are really not that expensive when you think of the alternative. Again, they can be worn on the body, placed in a purse or backpack, or hidden in a car. They can be used with children and the elderly, who may wander away from home.

These devices will tell you where your loved one is and where they are going. They can be programmed to sound an alert if a child wanders past a certain preset distance from you or the house. You can even see how fast the person is moving. If your child is supposed to be next door playing and is traveling at sixty mph, there is a problem.

The big "what IF!" I have heard people say, "what if the child removes or turns off the device?" That's just another excuse. Just teach them not do that. Everything you do as a family should be fully discussed and agreed upon. I have heard people say that if the child or person is snatched, the kidnapper will look for the GPS and throw it away. That's possible, but come on. What if they don't? The point is to try and protect your loved one. No more excuses.

As you have read, a cell phone can be used as a GPS device. *Every person in your household should have a cell phone for emergencies and know how to use it properly.* This includes children and teenagers.

Rule 10: Talk/Communicate - Sit down with your family and discuss the topic of personal and family security. Come up with a security plan. As explained earlier, there are videos and books for younger children that will teach them about "stranger danger" and personal security. With your older children, you are going to have to agree to certain rules. The more you talk about them, the more sense it will make to your children (younger and older). Let them talk as well, even if what they say is negative. Don't get frustrated. Just keep making your point. Nothing is worse than being physically beaten, raped, or murdered.

Rule 11: Make a plan and rehearse - Come up with various personal and family plans. Discuss these plans then rehearse various security scenarios and procedures. Military and police experts conduct what they call mental rehearsals. Develop various scenarios and rehearse them in your head. Discuss these scenarios and various solutions with others at home or in your group. You always need more than one plan. You need a contingency plan; should plan A fail, you have plan B as a back-up plan. Come up with multiple back-up plans. Again, train and rehearse different scenarios and techniques.

Your plans can include what should you do if you hear a possible breaking and entering? What do you do in the event of a hurricane, tornado, or any bad storm? You must also remember the very important fire drill. What does each person do if there is a fire in your home? Where will everyone meet? Where are your fire extinguishers? In the back of the book you will find various links. Kids Health.org even has individual sites for parents, teenagers, and children.

Then there are other plans. What do you do if you are being followed? What do you do if you have an accident? What do you do if someone contacts you on the telephone and starts asking personal questions? What do you do with your sensitive trash?

Rule 12: Social networking - If you use Facebook, MySpace, or any of the other social networks, including dating services, clean up your biographical information. Get it off the website or the company form.

CHAPTER 13: BASIC RULES TO FOLLOW

When I am required to provide a DOB, I just use a different one. Come up with a standard alternate DOB to use, or make sure you write it down. Same with your SSN.

Watch the pictures you post! Not only do these predators search these websites, but sometimes employers search them as well, meaning supervisors and Human Resources. You do not want your boss or employer seeing certain pictures.

Rule 13: Internet use - Parents and guardians, take charge of the Internet. If necessary, place the computer in a location where it can be openly observed, if your child or teenager cannot obey rules. This way you can monitor your children to see if they are playing violent games or surfing for pornography.

You can also set the restriction levels on the computer and make sure they are password protected. Same with your television.

You can even buy and install software that will capture all activities on the computer key stroke by key stroke and screen shot by screen shot. Again, do not do this just to spy, but use these programs if there is a *serious* issue of mistrust and abuse.

If you want to add any more rules, go ahead. Be creative. Think like a bad guy and think like a detective. Think like a parent.

I'm going to throw you this piece of advice: for those who travel anywhere overseas, I highly recommend you go online and check out the threat assessment of that country by the Department of State. Also review their guidance on safe travels. Upon your arrival, immediately check in with the nearest US embassy or consulate. If no one seems interested, use your newly acquired art of persuasion. They need to know where you are staying and what cities you will be visiting. Also provide them with your contact information. Obtain all their contact information as well.

Rule 14: Whatever you can think of yourself or learn through research.

Chapter 14

PERSONAL SECURITY EQUIPMENT AND SERVICES

Contact these companies to discuss and purchase equipment and devices for your personal security. This includes your home and your vehicles, even your place of work or school. I had a friend who owns his own business and was attacked at work. We discussed problems with his alarm system and installing cameras. He supposedly called his alarm company, but months later I saw no changes and I talked to him about installing his own equipment, since it was less costly.

These companies are not listed in alphabetical order. I suggest that if you do anything, consider the following: Get an alarm system for your home and business. Purchase the monitoring service. Do the same for your car or vehicle. Buy a personal GPS tracking device for your family members and purchase the monitoring service. There are other security devices and equipment to consider for home and travel. One in particular is the door bars for your sliding glass doors and regular doors.

ADT security:

ADT is a leading company for alarm systems and monitoring, both at home and for businesses. I was very pleased with my sales representative and the service they have provided to me and my family over the years.

When they come to your house, and after you have verified the technician at your door, ask a lot of questions. Remember what you have read. Always ask a lot of questions and always try to verify answers. Write down what you learn. Notes are important.

Visit: www.adt.com or phone 877-291-3604 or 866-746-7238 and speak to a representative.

Brick House Security:

Brick House Security has most everything you need to protect yourself, your family, your home, and your business. Their prices are extremely reasonable and they have policies for a thirty-day return and a ninety-day guarantee. Not to mention they provide excellent technical support for the products you purchase. I have found the sales representatives to be very helpful over the telephone. They will describe the various equipment and devices you are interested in and make recommendations. You really need to check out their impressive website.

Visit: www.brickhousesecurity.com or phone 1-800-654-7966

OnStar:

OnStar provides a variety of services for your car, with the most important being emergency assistance, navigation, and communications connectivity. If you need help, just push a button and start talking to a live person. If you are involved in a crash, OnStar can instantly recognize this and dispatch emergency services to your exact location.

CHAPTER 14: PERSONAL SECURITY EQUIPMENT AND SERVICES

You can also program the OnStar emergency number into your cell phone. There is so much information on OnStar that you need to browse their website and then call a representative—to do what? To ask a lot of questions.

Visit: www.onstar.com or phone 1-800-488-6348.

Amber Alert GPS:

Visit: www.amberalertgps.com or phone 1-888-334-3958

My Precious Kid:

Visit: www.mypreciouskid.com or phone 1-503-693-2832

Toothprints:

Visit: www.toothprints.info

Kids Health:

Visit: www.kidshealth.org

Child Help Organization:

Visit: www.childhelp.org

Life 360:

Visit: www.life360.com or phone 1-866-277-2233

Work Place Violence:

Visit: http://www.osha.gov/SLTC/workplaceviolence/

Dark Psychology – Criminal Minds and iPredators:

Visit: www.darkpsychology.co (not.com)

Dangers of Internet Dating:

Visit: www.dangersofinternetdating.com

Dangers on the Internet:

Visit: www.perverted-justice.com

Lt. Col. Dave Grossman:

Visit: www.killology.com/article_trainedtokill.htm

Kids Health:

Visit: www.kidshealth.org. Fire Safety: http://kidshealth.org/kid/watch/er/fire_safety.html

National Child Identification Program:

Visit: www.childidprogram.com or phone 1-972-934-2211

For Fires:

Visit: www.wikihow.com/Keep-Safe-During-a-House-Fire

Safety Cops.com:

Visit: www.safetycops.com. Stranger Danger: www.safetycops.com/stranger_danger.htm

CHAPTER 14: PERSONAL SECURITY EQUIPMENT AND SERVICES

I noted that the NCMEC did not believe in the Danger Stranger training theory for various reasons. I agree we should not teach our kids to be scared of "all" strangers; and that strangers may actually be LEO, EMS or a rescuer. Teaching children a simple phrase is not productive. As I have said, you must sit down with children and fully discuss all these issues and train with them. Don't teach them to be paranoid, but teach them to be smart.

However, I have found "some" of the information on this website, and similar Stranger Danger programs, to be very important. Establishing a code word for your children can be important. Strangers should never stop and ask kids for directions or engage them in a conversation. As a parent, there are many topics we must research and carefully consider. Google; "*Dateline NBC Stranger Danger*" to see a number of good videos on this topic. Visit SafetyCops.com for information on various topics.

Great Call:

Great Call offers a variety or emergency devices to include Jitterbug and 5Star Urgent Response. Please take a look at this website and their products and services.

Visit: www.greatcall.com or call 1-800-918-8543

CYBERsitter:

CYBERsitter has been around for over fifteen years and provides user-friendly software that will allow you to restrict objectionable information and monitor activities on your computer and the Internet. This includes social media such as Facebook, chat rooms, etc.

Again, please don't use this software to arbitrarily spy on your loved ones or others. Use it if there is a serious issue of mistrust or abuse.

Visit: www.cybersitter.com or phone 1-800-388-2761 for computer-monitoring software and more.

Net Nanny:

Net Nanny provides the same computer monitoring capabilities as CYBERsitter.

Visit: www.netnanny.com or phone 1-800-508-3600

US Consumers Product Safety Commission:

Visit: www.cpsc.gov

Chapter 15

WHO TO CONTACT FOR MORE INFORMATION AND HELP

Emergency:

Call 911. Or call your local police department or sheriff's office.

Make sure you know how to call 911 from your cellular telephone when traveling through different states. Make sure you store their main and/or nonemergency numbers in your home telephone directory and on all your cellular telephones.

To educate children on how to call 911, visit the following websites:

www.911forkids.com

http://kidshealth.org/parent/firstaid_safe/emergencies/911.html

Federal Bureau of Investigation (FBI):

Call (202) 324-3000 or visit www.fbi.gov

A Parent's Guide to Internet Safety

Visit: http://www.fbi.gov/stats-services/publications/parent-guide

Cyber Crimes

Visit: http://www.fbi.gov/about-us/investigate/cyber/cyber

The Internet Crime Complaint Center (IC3) in partnership between the FBI

Visit: http://www.ic3.gov/default.aspx

Department of Homeland Security, Homeland Security Investigations (HSI):

Call 1-800-DHS-2-ICE (1-800-347-2423)

Or visit: www.ice.gov/about/offices/homeland-security-investigations

Immigration and Customs Enforcement: (Cyber Crimes Center (C3)

Visit: www.ice.gov/cyber-crimes/

Customs and Border Protection (CBP):

Call 1-800-BE-ALERT (1-800-231-5378) or visit www.cbp.gov

US Border Patrol (USBP): (USBP is part of CBP)

CHAPTER 15: WHO TO CONTACT FOR MORE INFORMATION AND HELP

Call 1-800-BE-ALERT (1-800-231-5378)

Or visit: www.cbp.gov/xp/cgov/border_security/border_patrol/

US Department of State: (Office of Children's Issues)

Call (202) 647-4000. Hotline: 1-888-407-4747 or visit: www.state.gov

Sex Offender Websites:

www.fbi.gov/hq/cid/cac/registery.htm (Will direct you to your state, but has other information.)

www.ice.gov/pi/childexploitation/index.htm (Information on child exploitation.)

http://sexoffender.ncdoj.gov and www.doc.state.nc.us/offenders

(Example for North Carolina. Check your own state for more information. Note that most government websites will end with .gov or .us)

National Center for Missing and Exploited Children (NCMEC):

Visit NCMEC to help find missing children in the United States and internationally.

Contact the call center by telephone or talk to a specialist online if your computer is equipped with a microphone and speakers. Use your wireless cellular phone as well.

Learn more about the *Amber Alert* (national and local alert), *Code Adam* (shopping centers and other businesses), *CyberTipline* (child exploitation), *NetSmartz.org* (Internet awareness), *Child Victim Identification Program-CVIP* (child pornography identification), *INHOPE.org* (international Internet),

Child-Care Provider program and more. Find out more about the roles of law enforcement, media, attorneys, and others.

Call 1-800-The Lost (1-800-843-5678) or visit: www.missingkids.com and www.cybertipline.com

InHope:

InHope is the International Association of Internet Hotlines and coordinates a network of Internet hotlines all over the world, supporting them in responding to reports of illegal content to make the Internet safer.

It is located in The Netherlands. Visit www.inhope.org or visit NCMEC at www.missingkids.com

Let's Bring Them Home (LBTH):

Visit Let's Bring Them Home for support in finding a missing adult. LBTH also supports missing children efforts. You can learn about education and other programs as well. In 2009, LBTH absorbed the National Center for Missing Adults (NCMA).

Learn more about DOJ's National Missing-Person and Unidentified Persons System (NamUs).

Please consider supporting and donating to this charitable organization.

Call 1-800-690-FIND or (1-800-690-3463) or visit: www.lbth.org

Klaas Kids Foundation:

The Klaas Kids Foundation was established in 1994 to help prevent crimes against children. You can visit this website to learn more about this

CHAPTER 15: WHO TO CONTACT FOR MORE INFORMATION AND HELP

foundation, other programs, statistics, and laws. You can also visit their sister website, Beyond Missing. This is a program to help find missing children.

Please consider supporting and making a donation to support these two charitable organizations.

Call (415) 339-0293 or visit: www.**klaaskids.org** and their sister website: www.**beyondmissing**.com

Polly Klaas Foundation:

The Polly Klaas Foundation is a national nonprofit dedicated to the safety of all children, the recovery of missing children, and public policies that keep children safe in their communities. They have a 24/7 hour hotline and publish and distribute child safety information to people around the world.

Please consider supporting and making a donation to support this charitable organization.

Call (800) 587-4357 or visit www.**pollyklaas.org**

Kristen Foundation:

The Kristen Foundation was founded in 1999 and dedicated to the safe return of missing and abducted adults everywhere. This is a program to help find missing adults. Please give them your support as well.

This foundation was started by Joan Petruski in honor of Kristen Modafferi. Kristen was a student at North Carolina State University and studying in San Francisco when she suddenly disappeared. You will find a report on the website about what to do should a loved one turn up missing. However, this book is more detailed. Finding a missing person through a law enforcement or private investigation is all about the details.

Visit their website at: www.kristenfoundation.org

Call (704) 996-5066 or e-mail: Help@KristenFoundation.org

The National Missing and Unidentified Persons System (NamUs):

Although the problem of missing persons and unidentified human remains in this country has existed for a long time, significant progress has been made in recent years. In 2003, the DNA Initiative was launched. The Office of Justice Program's (OJP) National Institute of Justice (NIJ) began funding major efforts to maximize the use of DNA technology in our criminal justice system. Much of NIJ's work has focused on developing tools to investigate and solve the cases of missing persons and unidentified decedents.

Call (202) 307-0703 or visit both: www.findthemissing.org and www.namus.gov.

National Center for Elder Abuse (NCEA):

The NCEA is directed by the US Administration on Aging. It is a national, state, and local organization that supports the elderly against abuse, neglect, and exploitation.

Call (800) 677-1116 or visit: www.ncea.aoa.gov

National Runaway Switchboard (NRS):

The NRS was established in 1971. It is a national organization that assists parents, runaways, and homeless children. Their services are provided twenty-four hours a day and are confidential.

Call 1-800-RUNAWAY (1-800-786-2929) or visit: www.1800runaway.org

CHAPTER 15: WHO TO CONTACT FOR MORE INFORMATION AND HELP

International Center for Missing and Exploited Children (ICMEC): In 1987, the ICMEC was established with the assistance of NCMEC. The ICMEC is leading a global movement to protect children from sexual exploitation and abduction.

Call NCMEC for support. Their information is listed above. Visit: www.icmec.org

Congress.org: (To identify your federal and state legislators/ representatives)

Visit www.congress.org. Type in your address and full zip code (first five, next four). If you do not know the additional four digits to your zip code, this site will guide you through the steps to find your full zip code. You will then be able to identify all your federal and state representatives along with their contact information.

Call them and ask them what they are doing to combat this serious epidemic and support law enforcement and these national organizations. Ask them if they are supporting any of these programs, and if not, why.

Remind them that the foreign aid, pork barrel, and other spending waste. Ask them why they cannot try and direct more money to this missing-person epidemic.

Back this up with a detailed letter or e-mail. Send them a copy of this book to read. Maybe it will wake them up. I'm sure they have loved ones they want to protect as well.

Keep in mind that if you contact a senator or house representative, you will usually speak with a legislative assistant, but you can ask to speak to your representative directly. If you can, make an appointment and visit with them in person. Give them your letter and a copy of this book.

Congressional representatives have an office in Washington, D.C., and they maintain one or more offices in their home state or district. Senators may have as many as two to six offices in their home state. You can schedule a visit when they are at their home office. When they do come back to their home state or district, they are often campaigning for money or reelection. Remind them you are a constituent and you can support them…or NOT.

National Domestic Violence Hotline:

The National Domestic Violence Hotline creates access by providing 24-hour support through advocacy, safety planning, resources and hope to everyone affected by domestic violence. The National Domestic Violence Hotline was established in 1996 as a component of the Violence Against Women Act (VAWA) passed by Congress. *The Hotline* is a nonprofit organization that provides crisis intervention, information and referral to victims of domestic violence, perpetrators, friends and families. *The Hotline* answers a variety of calls and is a resource for domestic violence advocates government officials, law enforcement agencies and the general public.

Call 1-80-799-7233 or visit: www.thehotline.org

Childhelp National Child Abuse Hotline:

The Childhelp National Child Abuse Hotline is dedicated to the prevention of child abuse. Serving the United States, its territories, and Canada, the Hotline is staffed 24 hours a day, 7 days a week with professional crisis counselors who, through interpreters, can provide assistance in 170 languages. The Hotline offers crisis intervention, information, literature, and referrals to thousands of emergency, social service, and support resources. All calls are anonymous and confidential.

Call 1-800-422-4453 or visit: www.childhelp.org

CHAPTER 15: WHO TO CONTACT FOR MORE INFORMATION AND HELP

Rape, Abuse & Incest National Network (RAINN):

RAINN is the nation's largest anti-sexual violence organization and was named one of "America's 100 Best Charities" by Worth magazine. RAINN created and operates the National Sexual Assault Hotline with more than 1,100 local rape crisis centers across the country and operates the DoD Safe Helpline for the Department of Defense. RAINN also carries out programs to prevent sexual violence, help victims and ensure that rapists are brought to justice.

Call 1-800-65-4673 or visit: www.rainn.org

National Alcoholism and Substance Abuse Information Center:

The National Alcoholism and Substance Abuse Information Center maintains a state-of-the-art national database of the leading alcohol rehab treatment and drug rehab treatment centers in the US and around the world for every level of treatment option from affordable to luxury.

Call 1-800-784-6776 or visit: www.addictioncareoptions.com/

Any Others: Write down the contact information here. Google to learn more.

Chapter 16

THE END

This is the end of the book, but it is ***just your starting point***. As commented, I could continue writing, but this will get you started on a solid security plan for yourself and those you love. It provides you with some security measures to take. Learn more through your own research.

First, you need to complete the Biographical Form(s) and then finish the rest of your Individual Protection Packet(s). Please do this as soon as possible and keep them updated. Make plenty of thumb drives to have available.

Second, make up your Emergency Identification Cards (EID). Carry one on you and store them where they will be needed at home, work, school, etc. Parents should keep a copy of their children's EID Cards close by.

Third, you need to determine which physical security measures you will take at home, work, school, and when you are in your car. For starters, keep the lights on outside your home and get an alarm system. Think about the other measures, especially the personal GPS. As you do your research, you may learn about other equipment and systems I didn't mention. There are a lot more items and services out there and they are improving every day.

Fourth, there are people and organizations to talk to. Program critical telephone numbers into everyone's telephones. Speaking of storing numbers on your cell phones, start loading pictures onto your smartphone and your computer for future use.

Fifth, if you decide to become a champion for the missing-person effort, get involved now. Convince others to form a working group—small or large.

There was a lot of information in this book, so you might want to read it again or use it as a reference. There is more to know, and it is up to all of us to learn as much as possible. It is a daunting task being responsible for the lives of our loved ones. Yet I can't think of anything more loving and fulfilling. For those who protect others as well, there is nothing more honorable.

Convince all your loved ones to read this book. If you have younger family members, you may want to buy some children's books and videos. At a minimum, research the National Center for Missing and Exploited Children and both Klaas organizations for training material. Please research the other websites and organizations listed in chapters 14 and 15.

Sit down with your loved ones and have a serious discussion about all of this information. Establish a good security plan and implement rules for the entire family. Decide what security systems and equipment are useful to you and your family, and then get them. Train and rehearse!

I am a Christian. If you are not religious, you may want to skip the next several paragraphs. It's your choice.

If you are a true Christian, you believe in God and that the Bible is God's Word. You believe the Bible contains the teachings of Jesus Christ. A true Christian does not pick and choose what parts of the Bible they want to believe. Interpretations of scriptures are a different matter, but as a true Christian you place your faith in God and the Bible, right?

Having said that, a religious survey indicated many Christians do not believe in Satan. Lucifer is very real and so are Heaven and Hell. Read The Bible. What don't you believe about Satan or the Bible?

The struggle between God and Satan won't end until the Evil One is conclusively defeated and eternally confined as the Bible promises. We are God's children and He loves us. Satan wants to hurt and punish God by attacking us, God's children. The Devil tries to tempt us—and he even tried to tempt Jesus. Avoid temptations, especially when they pertain to the abuses of alcohol, drugs, sex, violence, and the many other vices. No sense in trying to wade through quicksand. You won't make it!

Aside from tempting us, Satan does attack and harm us. There is, in fact, evil in this world, and even some Christians ignore this fact and keep their heads buried in the sand when it comes to protecting themselves and their families. These violent offenders and sexual predators who prey on innocent men, women, and children are nothing more than "evil." Sure, they may have psychological disorders, but the root problem is the evil in their hearts.

Listen, there are hundreds of thousands of rational and educated Christians in the military and law enforcement who have met these cruel and heartless monsters face to face. I have. The same can be said for some criminal psychiatrists and physiologists who are Christians, but many of them also have a scientific and clinical view of these monsters. We know the unspeakable evil such individuals are capable of. If you have never met someone like this you may find this hard to believe. Satan and evil exist and these monsters are evil. Once you meet one you will understand. I pray you will not cross paths.

We all must pray that God will protect us and our loved ones from Satan and his evil. Pray every day that God prevails in this struggle of good over evil. However, and this is my personal view: God expects us to be responsible and to take personal measures to protect ourselves and our family. That is why we take vaccinations and medicine; to protect ourselves. We take other security measures and precautions to protect ourselves from accidents. That is why *we* must take steps to protect ourselves and our families from these evil attacks. Don't ignore the safety and security of your loved ones and others by saying it is in God's hands, or God's plan. Satan has other plans for us.

God offers us salvation and redemption, but we are free to take different paths in life and make our own choices—right or wrong. We are God's children and many of us are His warriors. We must all struggle with temptations, and we must all be prepared to fight and defeat evil. Protect yourself and your loved ones, okay?

For those who continued reading, but are unsure of your faith or religion. Find God and accept Him and Jesus into your life now. Don't put it off any longer.

Stay safe and God bless you and your family.

Made in the USA
Charleston, SC
01 October 2012